An Early History *of* Malden

An Early History of MALDEN

Frank Russell

THE History PRESS

Published by The History Press
Charleston, SC
www.historypress.com

Copyright © 2018 by Malden Historical Society
All rights reserved

First published 2018

Manufactured in the United States

ISBN 9781467139410

Library of Congress Control Number: 2018932096

Notice: The information in this book is true and complete to the best of our knowledge. It is offered without guarantee on the part of the author or The History Press. The author and The History Press disclaim all liability in connection with the use of this book.

All rights reserved. No part of this book may be reproduced or transmitted in any form whatsoever without prior written permission from the publisher except in the case of brief quotations embodied in critical articles and reviews.

In memory of my father,
who would have liked it,
and for my mother,
who does.

CONTENTS

PREFACE

This book—a brief history of Malden, Massachusetts, through the turn of the twentieth century—is the culmination of a twenty-five-year hobby of speaking, writing and researching Malden's fascinating history. I believe it serves a need for a compact, readable and authoritative history of the city. The early history of Malden is well documented in Deloraine P. Corey's *History of Malden*, which remains the authoritative resource on Malden's early history. However, it only covers the period up through 1785. Moreover, topping out at 832 pages, few modern readers will have the appetite to read it from cover to cover. Ruth Randall's history of Malden, published in 1976, while readable, is notable for glaring omissions.

This book attempts to cover concisely some material treated in more detail in Corey's *History* while, at the same time, bringing together from multiple scattered sources a brief, authoritative history of Malden in the nineteenth century. Attention is given to topics not covered in Randall's book. While some of the material here is original research from primary sources, much of Malden's history in the nineteenth century is gleaned from references in secondary sources. I have attempted to synthesize this material into a readable narrative.

I have also tried to address Malden's history in the context of larger themes in American history, such as the movement for independence, abolitionism and women's suffrage. I think local history is most interesting, and most relevant, where it intersects major issues in American history. I have tried to show the role Malden and Malden people played in these events. Thus there are brief biographical sketches of some noteworthy Maldonians; undoubtedly there are some others that are not addressed here.

The book is amply footnoted to encourage readers to go beyond this book and explore these cited materials and to use them as a roadmap for further research—there are many more stories waiting to be told beyond those in this book.

If you enjoy this book, or history in general, join the Malden Historical Society; attend one of its meetings. It's a great group of people interested in preserving and sharing Malden's history. An application can be found on its website (www.maldenhistoricalsociety.org).

I am grateful to the board of directors of the Malden Historical Society for permission to reproduce many of the illustrations in this volume and for its support of this project. I also wish to thank Professor Richard D. Brown of the University of Connecticut, Dr. John Tramondozzi and Linda Thorsen of the Malden Historical Society and Dora St. Martin, director of the Malden Public Library, for their generous time in reviewing the draft manuscript and making helpful suggestions and corrections. Barbara Tolstrup and Edward Flaherty of the Historical Society also reviewed the text. The final content, of course, as well as any errors or omissions, is my own.

Welcome to the wonderful world of Malden history. I hope you will enjoy reading it as much as I have enjoyed writing it.

Chapter 1

MYSTIC SIDE

In 1629, when Lieutenant Ralph Sprague along with his brothers, Richard and William, and their party first followed the old Indian trail around what would later be called Wayte's Mount, Malden's only inhabitants were the remnants of a once-powerful tribe of the Pawtuckets, under the leadership of Wonohaquaham, or Sagamore John.[1] Wonohaquaham lived on what is today called the Island End River or Chelsea Creek. Previously, the tribe had been led by Nanapashemet, who made his home in what were then the broad marshes that stretched from present-day Linden through Revere to the sea. Nanapashemet moved from Rumney Marsh to a hill near the headwaters of the Mystic River, where he was slain in 1619. After Nanapashemet's demise, the tribe was ruled by his widow, the Squaw Sachem, and two of his sons, Wonohaquaham and Montowampate, who was also called Sagamore James. The Squaw Sachem sold a good bit of land to the early English settlers in Charlestown for some coats, wampum and corn. This parcel included present-day Malden.

In 1632, a smallpox epidemic claimed most of the remaining members of the tribe, including Wonohaquaham and Montowampate. Their younger brother, Wenepoykin, said to be about seventeen, became the leader of the remaining Indians in the vicinity. Referred to by the English settlers as George Rumney Marsh, he lived near what was then the southern border of Malden, on Powder Horn Hill in present-day Everett. Wenepoykin appears to have lived peaceably with the early settlers of Malden until 1651, when he petitioned the General Court for the return of his "just title" to the lands of his brothers at Mystic Side. The petition was denied by the legislature with the admonition to proceed in court. After two court defeats, Wenepoykin was granted twenty acres of "good planting" for his use. Wenepoykin joined in the 1676 rebellion known as King Philip's War, during which he was taken prisoner and sent to slavery in Barbados. Around the same time, the remaining Indians moved to the Pawtucket Falls at Wamesit, near present-day Lowell. Somehow, Wenepoykin returned to Massachusetts, where he died in 1684 at the house of his nephew Muminquash (James Rumney Marsh) at Natick.

Soon after the Sprague brothers passed through present-day Malden, the area began to attract English settlers. Thomas Coytemore built a dam on the Spot Pond Brook[2] and set up a gristmill near the present-day intersection of Pleasant and Middlesex Streets. In 1640, Coytemore received a grant of five thousand acres of land, including the rights to Spot Pond in Charlestown (now Stoneham).[3] Coytemore was a mariner and an early pioneer in the developing maritime commerce of New England. He commanded a ship, the *Trial*, which sailed from Boston in 1642, loaded with fish and pipe staves, which he traded for wine and sugar in Faial in the Azores that he then took to the West Indies and traded for tobacco, cotton and iron. After a seven-month journey of more than 7,250 miles, Coytemore and the *Trial* returned to Boston in March 1643. Upon Coytemore's return, John Winthrop noted in his journal that "through the Lord's blessing they made a good voyage, which did much encourage the merchants, and made wine and sugar and cotton very plentiful, and cheap, in the country."[4] Coytemore was on the ship *Seafort* when it ran aground, and he perished off the coast of Spain in 1645.[5]

Coytemore left his widow, Martha, a sizeable estate. In December 1647, Martha became the fourth wife of John Winthrop, the first governor of the Massachusetts Bay Colony, but not before ensuring that the property she inherited from Thomas would remain hers, an early version of a prenuptial agreement.[6] This estate included not only the mill but also most of the land from the present-day high school and Pleasant Street up to Wayte's Mount, as well as water rights extending up Spot Pond Brook to Spot Pond.[7] After Winthrop's death, Martha married again in 1652, this time to wealthy Boston merchant John Coggan.[8] Coggan died in 1658 and left Martha, only forty-one, depressed and lonely. She apparently committed suicide in October 1660 by taking a great quantity of ratsbane.[9] The development of Coytemore's mill indicated the presence of a growing community. The inhabitants of the area north of the Mystic River, from Mystic Side to Reading, would take their wheat and corn to this mill to be ground.

Early settlers usually arrived at the landing place at Sandy Bank on the Malden River, near the present Bell Rock Cemetery, there being no convenient land route to Boston at the time. Before 1640, the only road appears to have been Salem Street, then called the Salem path, which ran to a ford in the Mystic River in Medford. In 1640, the Penny Ferry was established, allowing ferry travel across the Mystic River from Malden to Charlestown. The road to Penny Ferry ran along the edge of the marshes between the burying ground and the Mystic River; a portion of it survives today as Madison Street. A road from Reading to the Winnisimmet ferry at Chelsea was laid out in 1653.

In 1638, Joseph Hills; his wife, Rose; and his son-in-law, John Waite, arrived. John Greenland received a grant in 1640 "to plant upon a five acre lot in Charlestown bounds on Mistick Side." With them came other settlers from the main settlement at Charlestown, and they gradually pushed north and occupied the valley between Wayte's Mount on the east and the Spot Pond Brook on the west.

Chapter 2

A TOWN CALLED MAULDON

Separation by the Mystic River made worshiping at the church at Charlestown difficult for the English settlers north of the Mystic River at Mystic Side. As early as 1643, William Sargeant, a haberdasher and preacher, was at Mystic Side and ministered to the settlers. These Mystic Side settlers sought an independent church and separation from Charlestown. On May 2, 1649, the Court of Assistants voted "[u]pon the petition of Mistick-side men, they are granted to be a distinct towne, and the name thereof to be called Mauldon." Joseph Hills is said to have given Malden its name to honor his hometown, the ancient borough of Maldon, England. Although the origin of the name Malden is not certain, it is believed to be derived from two Saxon words: *mael*, meaning a cross, and *dune*, a hill. The city of Malden preserves the ancient connection: the three lions on the city seal represent those from the seal of the borough of Maldon, England.

Joseph Hills was a leading man in the Massachusetts Bay colony and important in the town. He was Speaker of the House of Deputies in 1647. In 1648, he completed the revision of Massachusetts laws that resulted in the first published code of laws in New England.[10] His home was at the corner of Main and Salem Streets, where the First Baptist Church is now located; a memorial boulder marks the spot.

Malden had briefly begun to enjoy its newfound existence when the townsfolk faced a dispute involving their pastor, Marmaduke Matthews. Matthews's sermons did not sit well with popular opinion at the time. As a result, the civil authorities brought censure of Matthews in a controversy that had at its center the rights of individual thought and expression and the independence of the church from interference by secular authorities. So great was the controversy that it caused a band of Malden women to petition the General Court on Matthews's behalf in a time when such action on the part of women was largely unheard of. Thirty-six Malden women signed the petition presented to the General Court:

> *To the Honored Court: The petition of Many Inhabitants of Maldon & Charlestown on Mysticside humbly shewith that the almighty God in great mercy to our souls as we trust hath after many prayer endeavors & long waiting brought Mr. Matthews among us & put him into the work of the Ministry. By whose pious life & Labors the lord hath afforded us Many Saving Convictions directions and Consolations whose Continuance in the Service of Christ if it were the good pleasure of god we much desire, And it is our humble Request to this Honored Court that you would please to pass by Some personal & particular failings (which may as we humbly conceive be your Glory & no grief of heart to you in time to come) And to permit him to employ those talents God hath furnished him with. So shall we your humble petitioners with many others be Bound to pray, etc.* 28.8.51.

Mrs. Sergeant	*Sarah Bucknam*	*Eliz. Mirrable*
Joan Sprague	*Thankslord Shepprd*	*Sarah Osburn*
Jane Learned	*Ffran. Cooke*	*An Hett*
Eliz. Carrington	*Eliz. Knoher*	*Mary Pratt*
Bridget Squire	*Bridget Dexter*	*Eliz. Green*
Mary Wayte	*Lyda Greenland*	*Joan Chadwick*
Sarah Hills	*Margrt Pemrton*	*Margrt Green*
An: Bibble	*Han. Whittamore*	*Helen Luddington*
Eliz. Green	*Eliz. Green*	*Susan Wilkinson*
Wid: Blancher	*Mary Rust*	*Joana Call*
Eliz. Addams	*Eliz. Grover*	*Rachel Attwood*
Han. Barret	*Margt Welding*	*Rebec. Hills*[11]

Ultimately, the General Court ordered the town to remove Matthews as minister, and he returned to his native Swansea, England.

After Matthews's departure, Malden gained a minister who became its most noteworthy colonial citizen: Michael Wigglesworth. Wigglesworth came to Malden at age twenty-two after graduation from Harvard College at the head of his class in 1651. He is reported to have preached in Malden

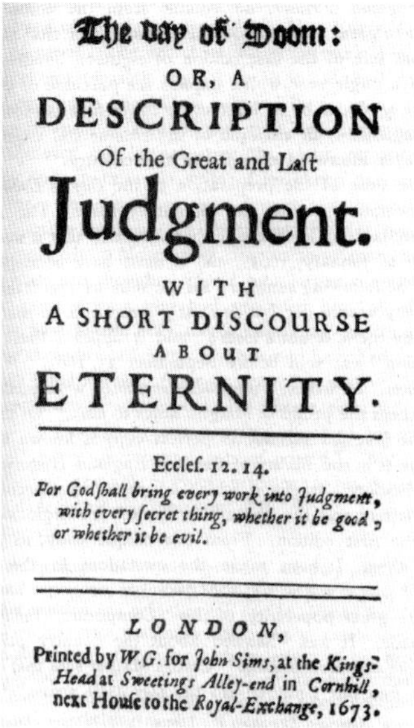

The day of Doom:
OR, A
DESCRIPTION
Of the Great and Laſt
Judgment.
WITH
A SHORT DISCOURSE
ABOUT
ETERNITY.

Eccleſ. 12. 14.
For God ſhall bring every work into Judgment, with every ſecret thing, whether it be good, or whether it be evil.

LONDON,
Printed by *W.G.* for *John Sims*, at the *Kings-Head* at *Sweetings Alley-end* in *Cornhill*, next Houſe to the *Royal-Exchange*, 1673.

Title page of Michael Wigglesworth's poem *The Day of Doom*. *Malden Historical Society.*

as early as 1654. Wigglesworth was a sickly man, and for a long period of time between ages twenty-one and twenty-eight, he is supposed to have been unable to attend to his ministerial duties and so turned his attention to writing. His poem *The Day of Doom* is studied by students of American literature today as a fine example of Puritan rhetoric. At the time, *The Day of Doom* and another poem, *Meat Out of the Eater*, attained a popularity akin to popular novels or films today. He was at one time offered the presidency of Harvard College. Wigglesworth died on June 10, 1705, beloved as "Maulden's Physician for Sole and Body Two," and is interred in the Bell Rock Cemetery.[12] Cotton Mather preached his funeral sermon.[13]

At this time, the majority of Malden's men were small farmers assisted at home by their wives and children. There was little industry in Malden at the time but for the Coytemore mill, which was rented by Abraham Hill from 1646 to 1656 after Coytemore's death. By the 1690s, James Harvell was operating his mill on Harvell's Brook on the easterly side of present-day Cross Street.[14] In 1651, the selectmen petitioned the General Court to allow Thomas Skinner to keep a tavern. With the area lacking an inn, in 1657 Abraham Hill was licensed to keep a tavern and draw wine to serve the church and neighboring country.

Meanwhile, Malden's roughly three hundred English settlers were earning an unsavory reputation, engaging in "slanders, assaults, domestic broils and other evils," mostly by charging one another with sexual misconduct. "Outsiders' comments on Malden broils demonstrate that it was atypical of the country and the colony as a whole," wrote historian Roger Thompson. From 1649 to 1699, sixty sexual misdemeanors were prosecuted in Malden—the colony's fifth-highest sex crime rate.[15] "One of the most notorious village Lotharios," Thompson noted, "was a Malden carpenter in his 50s, William Bucknam." His wife, Sarah, had been accused herself of sexual improprieties in the 1650s. William was charged in 1662 with "shameful lasciviousness" in word and deed toward fourteen married women. For example, Elizabeth Payne of Malden charged that Bucknam "puld me into his lapp and there held me and would not let me goe but kist me severall tymes." He was convicted and fined twenty-five pounds.[16] In 1685, Payne herself was charged with libel, for publishing "a kind of rhyme" making fun of Reverend Michael Wigglesworth. She was acquitted.[17] The Bucknam family pastime was apparently continued by William and Sarah's daughter-in-law, Sarah, who was convicted in 1676 of "unlawful and uncivill accompanying"—lying in bed with a Charlestown man. She and the man were given the harsh sentence of thirty-nine lashes each.[18]

In the 1670s, fears about King Philip and the Indians began to prevail among the population—fears that were realized in 1675. In October of that year, Malden was levied £15, 10s to support the expense of troops fighting Philip's army. Several townsmen served under Lieutenant William Hasey of Rumney Marsh, commander of the Three County Troop. In December 1675, seven Malden men fought in the Narragansett swamp fight under Captain Samuel Mosley. Edmund Chamberlain was killed and James Chadwick wounded. Another Malden soldier, Lieutenant Phineas Upham, died of wounds sustained in the great swamp fight. A total of twenty-nine men from Malden served in King Philip's War.

King Philip's War engendered much suffering and hardship for the colonists in the frontier towns but also for the Indians. Many of them were converted to Christianity by John Eliot. These so-called praying Indians were incarcerated at Deer Island by order of a mistrustful colonial government. It is likely that some of these unfortunates passed through or near the southern portion of Malden or Mystic Side on their way to Deer Island. That Malden townsfolk felt threatened by their presence is obvious. One of their numbers acted on his fears. In February 1676, Abraham Hill hatched a plan with Thomas Shepard to take thirty men from Charlestown, Malden and Lynn to Deer Island on a moonlight night to kill as many Indians as possible. The plan was never carried out, as Shepard's good sense compelled him to alert the authorities.[19]

In 1689, Malden men were among the mob that overthrew autocratic governor Edmund Andros. Returning to Malden, the men met in town meeting and called on the charter officers who had been unilaterally replaced by Andros three years earlier to resume their rightful offices. A precursor to Malden's action nearly a century later, the town meeting voted to "aid and assist them to the utmost of our Power with our Persons and estates."

Although relatively quiet, Malden did not entirely escape the tumult that was the witchcraft hysteria of 1692. Elizabeth Fosdick of Malden and Elizabeth Payne of Mystic Side were arrested and held in the Salem jail on charges of witchcraft. It was alleged they practiced witchcraft on Mercy Lewis and Mary Warren of Salem Village. Peter Tufts complained that they practiced witchcraft on his black female slave. Captain John Floyd was also arrested and imprisoned. The hysteria passed, and the accused were set free with other prisoners. Payne settled back into her practice as Malden's midwife.[20]

In 1663, William Godden left the residue of his estate for the purpose of educating the poor children of Charlestown and Malden. No early records survive as to schools, but it is known that a school was kept by the town in 1671. Apparently at the time, education was not a town priority, for the town was sporadically brought before the courts on charges that it failed to maintain a school. Ezekiel Jenkins came as schoolmaster in 1691 and served intermittently until 1705. Perhaps his job was not easy. His grave in the Bell Rock Cemetery is inscribed, "Mauldens Late School Master from a Painful Life Is Gone to Take His Rest Whome." Jenkins originally held session in his home, but by 1703, the school was kept in the town's watchhouse. It was not until 1712 that the town erected a schoolhouse, near the corner of present-day Pleasant and Main Streets. Schoolmasters were retained intermittently until Nathaniel Jenkins arrived in 1781. Reputed to be a vigorous disciplinarian, Jenkins taught for nearly twenty-five years.

Joseph Emerson was born in 1700 and entered Harvard College at age thirteen. Upon graduating in 1717, he began to preach and was ordained at Malden when he was only twenty-one years old. Emerson remained in Malden for forty-six years until his death in 1767.[21] Unlike Wigglesworth, Emerson's health was so good that tradition says he missed only two Sundays during his tenure as Malden's pastor. He is remembered on his gravestone as "learned, pious, and faithful." Emerson was noted as a capable preacher and was able to attract to Malden at least one of the great evangelicals of the day. On October 6, 1740, Reverend George Whitfield traveled to Malden at Emerson's request to preach here. Whitfield's revivalist meetings in 1740 led to the second phase of the "Great Awakening," a colonial religious revival.[22] At Emerson's request, Whitfield returned again on December 10, 1744. Whitfield's final sermon in Malden was August 19, 1770, where it said the meetinghouse was so packed that Whitfield had to make his way to the pulpit by way of a ladder through the back of the meetinghouse.[23] Emerson was the great-grandfather of the transcendentalist Ralph Waldo Emerson. Joseph Emerson was a noted scholar and accumulated a considerable library for those days. Emerson's pastorate, however, was not without difficulty.

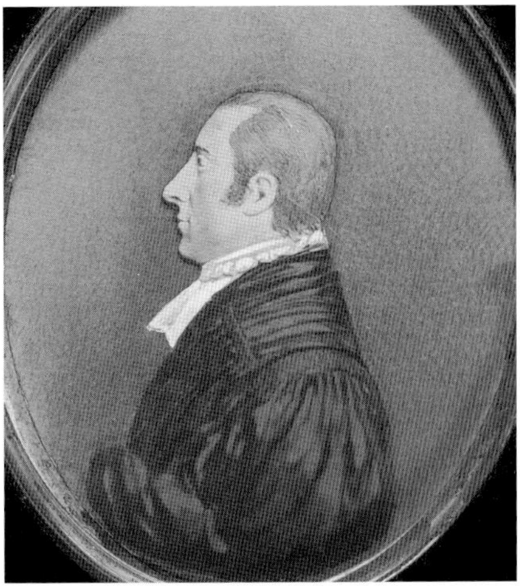

Reverend Joseph Emerson. Emerson was Malden's pastor from 1721 to 1767. *Massachusetts Historical Society.*

The first controversy concerned the location of the town's meetinghouse. Not surprisingly, the meetinghouse at Bell Rock had grown too small for the town. In 1727, a proposal was made for a new meetinghouse, and two locations were selected: one on town land near the Bell Rock meetinghouse and another site on the parsonage orchard. The town, however, opted for a third site located more northerly on Main Street between Lewis's Bridge, which was located on Main Street near present-day Eastern Avenue, and the town pound, which was located near the intersection of present-day Main and Pleasant Streets. Since this location was farther north, objections were raised from the southern portion of the town.

The dispute was ultimately settled by the General Court, which ordered the meetinghouse be built at the town's chosen location. This meetinghouse was completed in 1730, and Emerson gave its inaugural sermon on August 16, 1730. However, within four weeks, residents of the southern part of the town were organizing their own services, despite the town's claim that the new location was more accessible for these residents. Although they did not attend services, these residents were still obligated to pay support for Emerson's church. By 1733, southern residents were petitioning to be set off as a separate town and had organized the South Church. The issue simmered until 1737, when the legislature divided Malden into two precincts "for the promotion of religion and the peace of the town." The South Precinct survived for fifty-eight years.

Emerson's second difficulty was the July 1724 burning of the parsonage that he inhabited. Emerson lost not only his house but also the major part of his significant library and his furniture. The town moved with alacrity and had completed a new parsonage by January 1725.

Emerson died in 1767. After his death, his widow, Mary Emerson, became known as Madame Emerson. Shortly after the Revolution began, Madame Emerson's two-year-old granddaughter was sent to Malden to live with her and her insane aunt, Ruth. This infant was Mary Moody Emerson, the

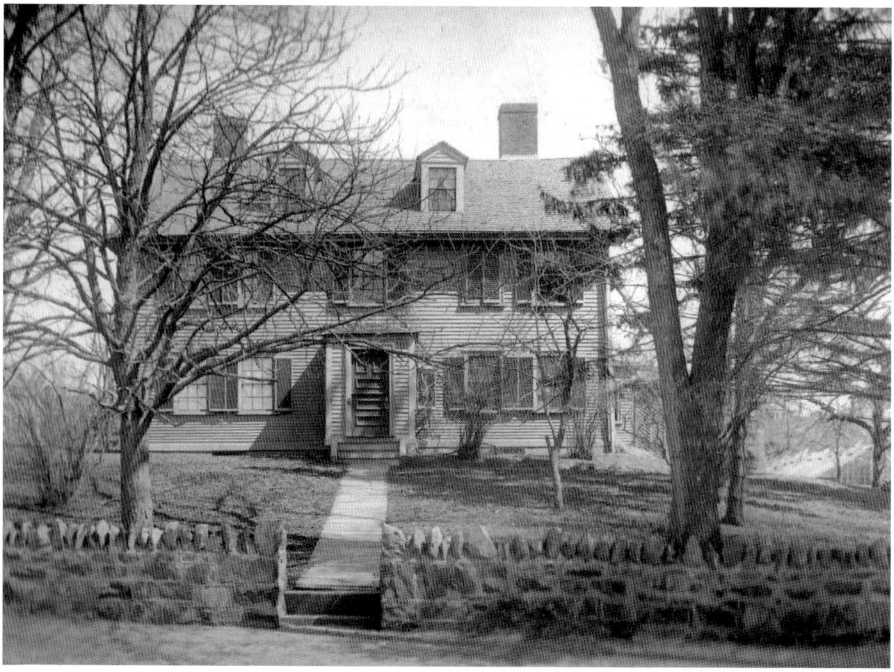

The parsonage at 145 Main Street opposite Bell Rock Memorial Park. Built in 1724, it was the home of Reverend Joseph Emerson and the birthplace of Adoniram Judson and the twin artists Darius and Cyrus Cobb. *Malden Historical Society.*

future aunt of Ralph Waldo Emerson. Perhaps one of the most remarkable women to have lived in Malden, Mary Moody Emerson resided here until 1807, when she moved to Maine.[24] Although burdened with the care of her grandmother and aunt, she was a voracious reader. Her tastes favored intellectual literature from Byron to Plato. She was said to be a frequent visitor at Captain Dexter's and fond of long walks in the fields and woods that covered the area. Nonetheless, she wrote that her life in Malden was "a slavery of poverty & ignorance & long orphanship…and lonesome solitude." Ralph Waldo Emerson called her his "muse." As a boy, Ralph Waldo came with Mary Moody to Malden to visit the graves of his ancestors in Bell Rock Cemetery, where he "skipped about among the graves."[25]

The French and Indian War began in 1755 and lasted for eight years. Malden men took part, but no formal military company was organized here. Lieutenant Simon Wade was wounded at Crown Point and killed at the Battle of Fort William Henry. A company commanded by Dr. Ebenezer Marrow of Medford contained thirty-one Malden men, including

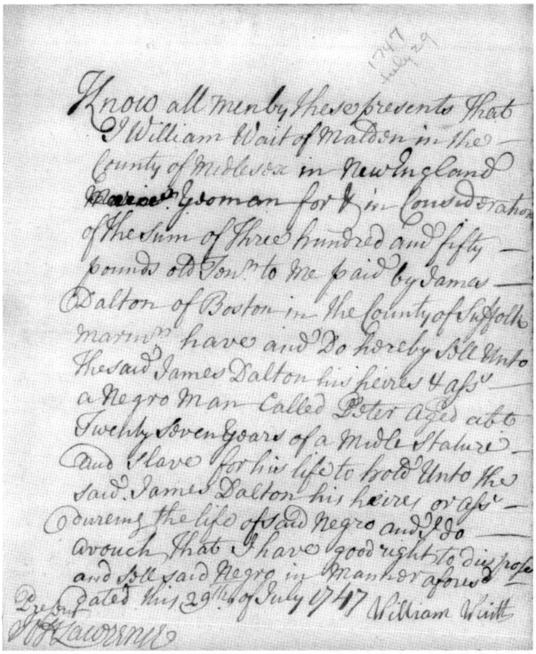

1747 July 29

Know all men by these presents That
I William Wait of Malden in the
County of Middlesex in New England
Yeoman for & in Consideration
of the Sum of Three hundred and fifty
pounds old Ten.r to me paid by James
Dalton of Boston in the County of Suffolk
marin.r have and Do hereby Sell Unto
the said James Dalton his heires & ass.s
a Negro Man Called Peter Aged ab.t
Twenty Seven Years of a Midle Stature
and Slave for his life to hold Unto the
said James Dalton his heires or ass.s
dureing the life of said Negro and I do
avouch that I have good right to dispose
and Sell said Negro in Manner afores.d
Dated this 29th of July 1747 William Waitt

Copy of deed from William Wait of Malden conveying a slave, Peter, to James Dalton of Boston in 1747. *Massachusetts Historical Society.*

Lieutenants Samuel Burditt and Darius Green of Malden. This company participated in the Battle of Ticonderoga, in which the colony's troops suffered heavy losses and sickness. Five Malden men—James Whittemore, John Burditt Jr., Ezekiel Floyd, Joseph Jenkins and Nathaniel Wayte—died in this battle. By 1758, the enrolled militia of Malden numbered 134 men under the command of Captain John Dexter.[26] This Dexter militia was the nascent beginning of Malden's Revolutionary War militia.

At the time of Reverend Emerson's death in 1767, Malden was predominantly a farming community, although there were at least seven workshops in the town. Livestock consisted of horses, oxen, cows, sheep and swine. Malden's farmers produced grain, hay and cider. Most of the hay was harvested from the salt marshes. There were artisans in the town, perhaps most prominent being the Lamson family, noted for their gravestone carvings.[27] Most travel was on foot and horseback. A 1759 account shows only one chaise and fourteen buggies in town. It was a small town of small means—mostly farms and a few industries.

Slavery existed in Malden, although not of the type or scale known in the southern colonies. Some of the known names are Brahma Bucknam, Cato Lynde, Phyllis Willis and Violet Hills. In 1742, deacon John Pratt valued his cow and an "oald neagroman" at the same value: £10 each. In 1747,

William Wait sold "a negroman named Peter aged abt twenty seven years" to James Dalton of Boston for £350 old tenor.[28] A 1768 inventory of Ezra Green's estate valued a slave named Jeffre at £20 and a boy named Simon at £33. Captain John Dexter was known to have had at least three slaves: Titus, Minerva and Cato.[29] The last known slave in Malden was Simon Knights, who remained in Malden until his death in 1847. Knights had belonged to Bernard Green and was later freed and became a member of the Baptist church. He lived in a house on Haskin's Lane, now Eastern Avenue, between Hillside Avenue and Main Street. Slavery was largely abolished in Massachusetts in 1783 by the Quock Walker case.[30]

Chapter 3

WE BID A FINAL ADIEU TO BRITAIN

Great Britain was in need of revenue in the 1760s and saw its colonies as an untapped resource. In early 1765, Lord Grenville introduced a measure in Parliament calling for a stamp tax on all newspapers, broadsides, pamphlets, licenses, commercial bills and legal documents.[31] The seemingly innocuous measure passed Parliament without difficulty; however, its reception in the colonies was unexpectedly violent.[32] In 1765, the townspeople of Malden joined in the protest against the hated Stamp Act. At a public town meeting held on October 17, 1765, the town voted that instructions be given to Captain Ebenezer Harnden, its representative in the General Court, as follows:

> *That you promote and readily join in such dutiful remonstrances and humble petitions to the King and Parliament…as may have a tendency to obtain a repeal of the Stamp Act and of the heavy burdens thereby imposed on the American British colonies. We are of the opinion that…the Stamp Act* [lays]*…a very burdensome and in our opinion unconstitutional tax… upon us all and we* [are] *subjected to numerous and enormous penalties.… These are our sentiments of the Stamp Act. We therefore, the inhabitants of said town, being legally assembled for this purpose, must enjoin it upon you not to comply with any measures or proposals countenancing the same or assisting in the execution of it; but by all lawful means consistent with our allegiance to the King and relations to Great Britain, to oppose the execution of it until we can hear the success of the cries and petitions of America for relief.*[33]

So spoke the town of Malden. With the Stamp Act, colonists, including those in Malden, began to form their views of their role in the British empire—the idea that they were not represented in Parliament directly.[34] Because of colonial opposition and boycotts of British goods, the Stamp Act was repealed in March 1776.[35]

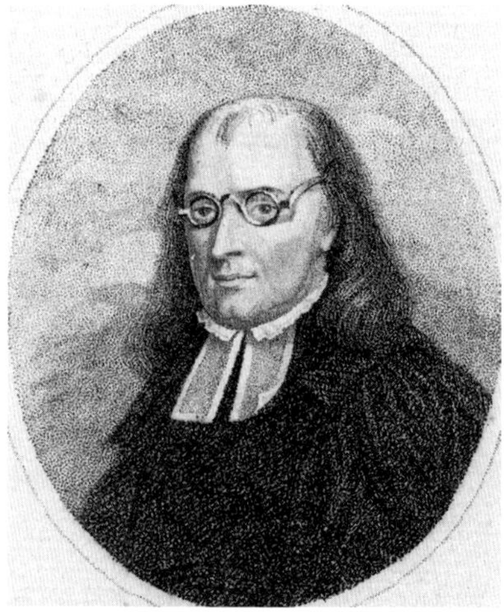

Reverend Peter Thacher became Malden's minister in 1770 at the age of eighteen. He authored Malden's instructions for independence. *Massachusetts Historical Society.*

Soon, the town of Malden would find a preacher who would give voice to its revolutionary feelings. After Emerson's death in 1767, it took the town three years to find a successor in the person of Peter Thacher. Thacher was ordained at the young age of eighteen. He was called "the young Elijah" by none other than the great preacher George Whitfield. Over the next few years, it would be Thacher's pen that would give voice to the sentiments of the town with respect to independence.

In opposition to the 1767 Townshend Act, Boston merchants entered into a non-importation agreement in August 1768.[36] In 1770, Malden voted resolutions in support of the nonimportation agreement. At the March 5, 1770 town meeting, it was voted "[t]hat we will not by ourselves or any for or under us, directly or indirectly purchase any Goods of any Person whatsoever, that continues to import the same contrary to the Agreement of the Merchants…[t]hat we will not use any foreign tea, nor Countenance the use of it in our Families (unless in Case of Sickness) till the Revenue Acts are repealed."[37]

In June 1774, the Boston Port Act closed the port of Boston and brought commerce to a virtual standstill. No doubt it caused hardship for the Malden farmers who brought their products to Medford that, along with bricks and rum from Medford, were transported down the Mystic River in small boats called lighters.[38] This must have influenced the sentiments of the town that manifested in a town meeting on September 23, 1774. There, the town adopted instructions to its representative, Captain Ebenezer Harnden, proclaiming their "firm, our deliberate resolution, rather to risque our lives and fortunes than to submit to these unrighteous acts of the British Parliament which pretend to regulate the government of this province...we are determined in the strength of our God, that we will, in spite of open force and private treachery, live and die as becomes the descendants of such ancestors as ours, who sacrificed their all, that they and their posterity might be free."[39]

Four days later, Malden's Committee of Correspondence met with other such committees from surrounding towns.[40] In response to the Port Act, the committees of these towns voted: "That should any person or persons... supply the troops now stationed in the town of Boston...with labor, lumber, joists, spars, pickets, straw, bricks, or any materials whatsoever, which may furnish them with requisites to annoy or in any way distress said inhabitants, he or they so offending shall be held in the highest detestation; be deemed the most inveterate enemies of this people; and ought to be prevented, opposed, and defeated, by all reasonable means whatsoever."[41]

The town's Committee of Correspondence was vigilant. Along with Chelsea's committee, it suspected Dr. Samuel Danforth of Loyalist sympathies because of his frequent travels to and from Boston and his removal of hay to Boston.[42] When four Malden residents who were suspected of similar sympathies—Ebenezer Pratt, John Nichols, John Barrett and John Nichols Jr.—obtained passes from British vice-admiral Graves in Boston, the committee met with the four but also notified the Committee of Safety in Cambridge of its concerns.[43] Indeed, monitoring suspected Loyalists who arrived in the town seems to have been a common occurrence.[44] Three suspected Loyalist women arrived in Malden from Boston. Colonel Loammi Baldwin had them placed under guard and taken to Watertown.[45] At one point, there was concern that the British intended to send persons ill from smallpox into surrounding towns to infect the populace.[46] When one person arrived in Malden from Boston with smallpox, no less than General George Washington was notified.[47]

Malden's militia was commanded by Captain Benjamin Blaney, a tanner by trade.[48] The militia became the subject of town ordinances, and drills were common. Blaney's regular company was placed on the alarm list as minutemen and numbered about one-quarter of the entire enrolled militia of the town.

On the morning of April 19, 1775, Paul Revere carried his famous alarm that the regulars were out to Medford. The Malden minutemen were then alerted by a rider dispatched from Medford who arrived in Malden in the wee morning hours.[49] This rider notified a Patriot leader in Malden who rang the town bell at Bell Rock, summoning the Malden minutemen to meet at Kettell's Tavern. From Malden, the alarm was carried to Chelsea.[50] The Malden minutemen mustered at Kettell's and marched with seventy-five men bearing the arms they used at Ticonderoga and bayonets purchased by Captain Dexter in 1758. Ordered to Watertown, they were intercepted by an officer who ordered them to Lexington. At West Cambridge, the Malden company came upon one of the regulars' provision trains and assisted in its capture, reportedly in conjunction with a company from Chelsea commanded by Reverend Phillips Payson and Samuel Sprague. The Malden men then joined in the pursuit of the regulars to Charlestown. Passing over Winter Hill, they were joined by a portion of the Essex company from Salem. Another portion of the Essex company arrived later and spent the night in Malden. Blaney and his men reached Charlestown neck at dusk and observed the rear guard of the regulars on the western slope of Bunker's Hill. Although Blaney and his men reached neither Lexington nor Concord, the town dispatched boys on horseback with saddlebags filled with supplies to replenish the militia in the field.[51] Another company commanded by Naler Hatch, made up of the alarm list of sixty men, was stationed at Sweetser's Point[52] during the day. In the evening, they returned to Malden, although a number of the men asked permission to go to Concord.[53]

Many inhabitants of Charlestown fled to Malden across the Penny Ferry and remained there during the siege. Two days after the battle, several field pieces were removed from Newburyport to Malden, where they were entrusted to Captain John Dexter. At the same time, orders forbade inhabitants of Malden and Chelsea from firing upon any seamen unless first fired upon by them. Soon after, this order was withdrawn, and the townspeople were told "to put themselves in the best state of defence and exert the same in such manner as under their circumstances their judgments may direct." Two companies, under the commands of Blaney and Captain Samuel Sprague of Chelsea, were raised for the defense of the seacoast of the two towns. This company participated in the Battle of Chelsea Creek on May 27–28, 1775, driving livestock from Noddle's Island and capturing twelve swivels and four small cannons.[54]

Malden formed another militia company under the command of Captain Naler Hatch. Hatch's company was stationed at Sweetser's Point in the southern part of town on June 17, 1775, the day of the Battle of Bunker's Hill, with a full view of the unfolding spectacle. Peter Thacher viewed the battle from this location and was appointed by the Committee of Safety to prepare an official account.[55] Patriot leaders promptly sent Thacher's narrative to Arthur Lee, the colonies' representative in London.[56] Aaron

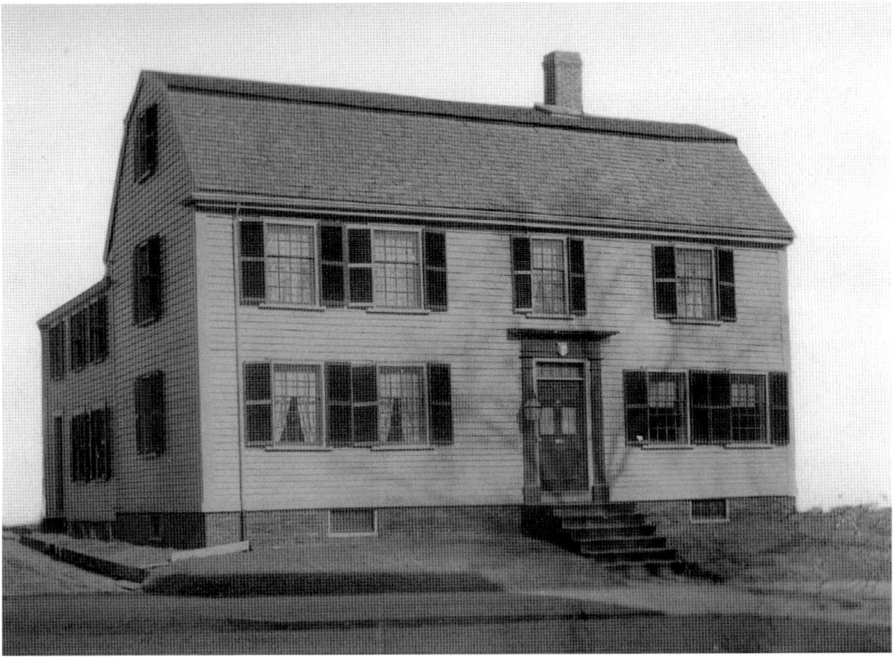

Hill's Tavern, also called Kettell's Tavern, was on Main Street opposite Pleasant Street. *Malden Historical Society.*

Dexter also recorded his views of the battle from the Malden side of the Mystic River.[57]

During the battle, residents of the southern portion of the town headed for safety, some as far as Reading. Others followed Salem Street to Black Ann's Corner and the hills of Maplewood Highlands, then called Scadan. Wayte's Mount served as a vantage point for townspeople to view the battle in safety.[58] Some of the wounded were brought to a tavern operated by Dr. Jonathan Porter on Salem Street. After the battle, the southern part of the town remained in the colonists' control. Malden men erected an earthen barrier at about the present intersection of Main and Bow Streets in what is today Everett. Hatch's company defended the southern part of Malden with assistance from a company from Essex commanded by Captain Eleazer Lindsey. Hatch would later go on to command a privateer, the *Lady Washington*.[59]

On August 6, 1775, the British crossed the Mystic River into Malden, landing at Penny Ferry and causing a stir among the lines. They burned a house, and according to some reports, Captain Lindsey and his men fled the scene. Damage to Malden property during this time was confined to the southern part of the town.

As the winter of 1775 approached, the defense of the Middlesex Fells, then called the Charlestown Wood Lots, became of paramount importance. Both armies needed wood for fuel in the winter, although the wood lots had been reserved for use in the Royal Navy by the king. It was feared that the British would cross the Mystic to obtain wood or stop the colonists from doing so. The local militia took some prisoners in this area.[60] No doubt the crossing of Mystic River and the defense of the wood lots were the impetus behind George Washington's visit in the fall of 1775 to view the entrenchments at Chelsea and Malden. He and his entourage also visited at Captain John Dexter's, where, legend says, one of Washington's officers knocked a stone off a stone wall. The officer intended to leave the replacement of the stone to someone else when Washington went and replaced the stone, remarking, "I always make it my rule when visiting a place to leave things in as good order as I find them."[61]

In the spring of 1776, independence was on the minds of the town and Reverend Thacher. Thacher received a singular honor when he was selected to give the Boston Massacre commemorative address in March 1776.[62] Thacher was in good company; previous orators had included Dr. Joseph Warren (1772 and 1775) and John Hancock (1774). His Boston Massacre oration presages the themes Thacher would use two months later in drafting Malden's instructions for independence:

> *MY FRIENDS, WHEN the ambition of Princes induces them to break over the sacred barriers of social compact, and to violate those rights, which it is their duty to defend, they will leave no methods unessayed to bring the people to acquiesce in their unjustifiable encroachments.... To fright us into submission to their unjustifiable claims, they sent a military force to the town of Boston. This day leads us to reflect upon the fatal effects of the measure! By their intercourse with troops, made up in general of the most abandoned of men, the morals of our youth were corrupted: The temples and the day of our God were scandalously prophaned: We experienced the most provoking insults; and at length saw the streets of Boston strewed with the corpses of five of its inhabitants, murdered in cool blood, by the British mercenaries....FINDING their arts insufficient to flatter, or their treasures to bribe the people of America, out of their freedom, the British government determined, by force, to subjugate them to their arbitrary will: In consequence of this determination, a large party of their troops marched from Boston, on the morning of the ever memorable nineteenth of April last, flushed with the hopes of*

certain victory, and defying the armies of the living God, they broke through every divine and political obligation; they wantoned in cruelty; they shed again American blood.... Aroused by the unprovoked injury, like a lion, awaking from his slumber, we sprang to arms! we felt ourselves inspired with the spirit of our ancestors, we heard our brethrens blood crying to us for vengeance, we rushed into the midst of battle: we compelled our enemies to betake themselves to a disgraceful flight, we pursued them with avidity, and desisted not till they took refuge in that city, of which, by fraud and treachery, they had possessed themselves.... That elation of spirit, which is excited by our victories, is damped by our feeling the calamities of war. To hear the expiring groans of our beloved countrymen; to behold the flames of our habitations, once the abodes of peace and plenty, ascending to Heaven, to see ruin and desolation spread over our fruitful villages, must occasion sensations in the highest degree painful...Freedom is offered to us, she invites us to accept her blessings; driven from the other regions of the globe, she wishes to find an asylum in the wilds of America; with open arms, let us receive the persecuted fair, let us imitate the example of our venerable ancestors, who loved and courted her into these desert climes. With determined bravery, let us resist the attacks of her impudent ravishers; by resolution and firmness we may defend her from their power, and transmit her blessings to millions upon millions of our posterity. Let us then arouse to arms! For, upon our exertions, under God, depends their freedom, upon our exertions depends the important question, whether the rising empire of America, shall be an empire of slaves or of freemen.... With transport, my countrymen, let us look forward to the bright day, which shall hail us a free and independent state. With earnestness let us implore the forgiveness and the patronage of the Being of all beings, who holds the fate of empires in his hands! With zeal let us exert ourselves in the service of our country, in life: And when the earthly scene shall be closing with us, let us expire with this prayer upon our quivering lips, O God, Let America Be Free![63]

On May 10, 1776, the Massachusetts Assembly asked the inhabitants of each town to advise their representatives whether the inhabitants would support Congress in the measure if the Continental Congress declared independence.[64] Malden, through Thacher's pen, was one of the first to lend its voice to the growing chorus for separation.[65] On May 27, 1776, a town meeting was held in response to a resolution of the Massachusetts House of Representatives asking towns to meet and advise and instruct their representatives on the question of independence. Peter Thacher authored the stirring instructions that Malden voted to send to its representative, Ezra Sargent:[66]

Sir—A resolution of the hon. house of representatives, calling upon the several towns in this colony to express their minds in respect to the important question of American independence, is the occasion of our now instructing you. The time was, sir, when we loved the king and the people of Great Britain with an affection truly filial; we felt ourselves interested in their glory; we shared in their joys and sorrows; we cheerfully poured out the fruit of all our labours into the lap of our mother country, and without reluctance expended our blood and treasure in their cause.

These were our sentiments toward Great Britain while she continued to act the part of a parent state; we felt ourselves happy in our connection with her, nor wished it to be dissolved; but our sentiments are altered, it is now the ardent wish of our soul that America may become a free and independent state.

A sense of unprovoked injuries will arouse the resentment of the most peaceful. Such injuries these colonies have received from Britain. Unjustifiable claims have been made by the king and his minions to tax us without our consent; these claims have been prosecuted in a manner cruel and unjust to the highest degree. The frantic policy of administration hath induced them to send fleets and armies to America; that, by depriving us of our trade, and cutting the throats of our brethren, they might awe us into submission, and erect a system of despotism in America, which should so far enlarge the influence of the crown as to enable it to rivet their shackles upon the people of Great Britain.

This plan was brought to a crisis upon the ever memorable nineteenth of April. We remember the fatal day! The expiring groans of our countrymen yet vibrate on or ears! And we now behold the flames of their peaceful dwellings ascending to Heaven! We hear their blood crying to us from the ground for vengeance! Charging us, as we value the peace of their names to have no further connection with a king—who can unfeelingly hear of the slaughter of—and composedly sleep with their blood upon his soul. The manner in which the war has been prosecuted hath confirmed us in these sentiments; piracy and murder, robbery and breach of faith, have been conspicuous in the conduct of the king's troops: defenceless towns have been attacked and destroyed: the ruins of Charlestown, which are daily in our view, daily reminds us of this: the cries of the widow and orphan demand our attention; they demand that the hand of pity should wipe the tear away from their eye, and that the sword of their country should avenge their wrongs. We long entertained hope that the spirit of the British nation would once more induce them to assert their own and our rights, and bring to condign punishment the elevated villains who have trampled upon the sacred rights of men and affronted the majesty of the people. We hoped in vain, they have lost their love of freedom, they have lost their spirit of just resentment; we therefore renounce with disdain our connection with a kingdom of slaves; we bid a final adieu to Britain.

Could an accommodation now be effected, we have reason to think that it would be fatal to the liberties of America; we should soon catch the contagion of venality and dissipation, which hath led Britains to lawless domination. Were we placed in the situation we were in 1763; were the powers of appointing to offices, and commanding the militia, in the hands of governors, our arts, trade and manufactures would be cramped; nay, more than this, the life of every man who has been active in the cause of his country would be endangered.

For these reasons, as well as many others which might be produced, we are confirmed in the opinion that the present age would be deficient in their duty to God, their posterity and themselves, if they do not establish an American republic. This is the only form of government which we wish to see established; for we can never be willingly subject to any other King than he who, being possessed of infinite wisdom, goodness and rectitude, is alone fit to possess unlimited power.

We have freely spoken our sentiments upon this important subject but we mean not to dictate, we have unbounded confidence in the wisdom & uprightness of the Continental Congress with pleasure we recollect that this affair is under their direction and we now instruct you Sir, to give them the strongest assurance that if they should declare America to be a free & independent republic your constituents will support and defend the measure to the last drop of their blood & the last farthing of their treasure.[67]

Thacher remained Malden's pastor until he received a call from the Brattle Street Church in Boston in 1785. His removal from Malden resulted in several letters of protest in the *Massachusetts Centinel* and in a letter from the Malden church to its Boston neighbor complaining that it had "wounded us in a tender part" and that "our distress, anxiety, and trouble are great indeed." During his pastorates in Malden and Boston, Thacher published numerous sermons. Thacher later went on to become one of the founders of the Massachusetts Historical Society, the oldest historical society in America.[68] He participated in drafting the Massachusetts Constitution of 1780. In 1794, he was elected a fellow of the American Academy of Arts and Sciences. He served the Brattle Street church until his death in 1802. William Emerson, the son of Joseph Emerson, preached his funeral sermon.[69]

After the British left Boston, Malden was generally remote from the dangers of the Revolution. However, in July 1776, it was ordered that the town erect a signal beacon to warn of any approach of enemy ships.[70] The beacon, with a sentry and a warning cannon, was installed at Wayte's Mount. Malden's men, however, were still at risk of life and limb in the service of independence. In the summer of 1776, twenty-nine Malden men were sent to reinforce Washington's army, which was attacking the enemy in New York. Nine Malden men served at the Battle of White Plains in October 1776, including Sergeant Bernard Green and Corporal Timothy Tufts. Captain Blaney and nine other men drafted from the Middlesex militia marched in December 1776 to join the Continental army. Thereafter the town repeatedly furnished its quota of men as requested.

One of the more notable Malden men in the Revolution was Daniel Waters. Waters was a mariner who resided in the south part of town where, for many years, a spring bore his name. He marched with Blaney on April 18. George Washington appointed him to command a gunboat on the Charles River in 1775. In January 1776, he was promoted to the schooner *Lee*, where he commanded about fifty men for a year. He distinguished himself by capturing several British transports. Washington appointed him a captain in the navy on March 15, 1777. In 1777, while captaining a prize, the *Hancock*, Waters was captured in Halifax and imprisoned in New York. With Waters released in a prisoner exchange in April 1778, the *Boston Gazette* of April 27, 1778, mentioned his return to Boston. By December 1779, Waters was in command of an armed privateer from Marblehead, the *Thorn*. On Christmas morning, the *Thorn* encountered the British brig *Tryon*. When the *Tryon* hailed the *Thorn* demanding to know why it was flying the thirteen stars in its pennant, Captain Waters is said to have replied, "I'll let you know presently," and proceeded to fire a short-range broadside into the British ship. The *Tryon* and its sister ship, the *Erskine*, engaged the *Thorn* for an hour an attempted to board it. Waters's men fought off the attack, and an eyewitness reported, "The British sailors were seen running about deck with pikes in their backs instead of their hands." The *Thorn* prevailed, and the *Erskine*, seeing defeat, fled. Waters pursued the *Erskine* for three hours and overtook it, and after some shots, it surrendered. Eighteen men in all were killed or wounded on the *Thorn*, and Waters was permanently injured in his right knee. After the Revolution, Waters retried to his farm in South Malden, where he died on March 26, 1816.

Jonathan Oakes commanded a vessel in the Revolution after a twenty-year career in the merchant service. Captaining the *Hawke* from 1776 to 1779, Oakes sailed with Waters to the disastrous expedition at Halifax, although he escaped capture. After brief commands of the *Thomas* and the *Favorite*, Oakes was granted a letter of marque and commanded the *Patty*, of which he was an owner. In April 1781, the *Patty* took the British brig *Betsey*. After the Revolution, Oakes continued in the mercantile trade and by 1796 was in Paris as agent for John and Richard Codman of Boston. Other Malden men in the naval service included physicians Dr. John Sprague and Dr. Ezra Green. Isaac Smith, Naler Hatch and Nathan Nichols also commended vessels. A total of 231 Malden men served on land or at sea in the Revolutionary War.

Chapter 4

THE PEOPLE ARE BRIDGE MAD

The town of Malden remained split into two parishes after independence: the original north parish, ministered by Peter Thacher, and the south parish, ministered by Eliakim Willis. After Thacher's departure from the north parish in 1785, it took the town eighteen months to settle on a new minister, Reverend Adoniram Judson. All was not smooth sailing, however, and Judson's arrival led to opposition among townspeople who saw him as an impediment to the reunification of the south parish with the original church. Indeed, when Captain John Dexter and twenty-one others signed a letter of protest and joined the south parish, Reverend Willis witnessed some life breathed into his congregation. Unable to soothe the discontent, Judson was dismissed from the pastorate in 1791. Judson's son, also named Adoniram Judson, was born in the parsonage on Main Street opposite Bell Rock Park on August 9, 1788. The younger Judson went on to become the first missionary to Burma.[71] Judson Square preserves his name.

After Judson's dismissal as pastor, Captain Dexter and his followers returned to the north parish, bringing with them Reverend Eliakim Willis and the long-sought reunification of the town as a single parish. Although the town was now unified in one church, soon more profound disputes arose that would forever change it.

Beginning during Judson's pastorate, some church members began to question the validity of infant baptism and embrace Baptist principles. An itinerant preacher, Samuel Shepard, arrived in 1797 and is believed to have preached the first Baptist sermon in the town in the Peter Tufts House on Cross Street. His success led to revival meetings and then regular Baptist services by 1800. These services were held in an old schoolhouse until opposition mounted from the established Malden church; the "schismatics," as they were called, were banned from meeting in the schoolhouse. Baptists then began to meet in Benjamin Faulkner's barn, where, in 1803, the First Baptist Church was organized with forty-two members. Baptisms were conducted in Malden Center, where the eddying of the Spot Pond Brook formed a pond just south of the intersection of Pleasant and Main Streets. Parishioners would gather at Hill's Tavern, cross Main Street to the pond to be baptized and return to Hill's to change their clothes and, in the winter, warm up.

In a vain attempt to counteract the organization of the Baptist society, Dr. David Osgood, a Medford minister, preached two sermons in Malden in defense of infant baptism that were subsequently printed and distributed.[72] Despite Osgood's efforts, Baptist members grew, and Baptists erected a meetinghouse on the site of the present-day Salem Street Cemetery in 1804. They would use it until 1843, when they acquired the site at the corner of Main and Salem Streets in Converse Square. For many years, Salem Street was informally referred to as "Baptist Row," not only because of Faulkner's barn and the Baptist meetinghouse but also because most in the vicinity were Baptists.[73]

Soon thereafter, another portion of the Malden church, mostly residents of North Malden, were drawn away from the parish by the formation of a Methodist society. A member of this society, James Howard, moved closer to Malden Center and, after a revival meeting, formed the Center Methodist Church.[74] Meetings were first held in Howard's house and later in a brick school. By 1825, the Methodists had grown sufficiently to erect a church on Main Street.

The growth of various religious societies in Malden, characteristic of the entire state, reflected growth in the developing town after the Revolution. Indeed, in need of enlarged meeting space, the Malden church erected a new brick meetinghouse on Main Street, opposite the site of present-day Sacred Hearts Church, in 1802. This, the town's fourth meetinghouse, was the town meeting hall in all respects. The eccentric "Lord" Timothy Dexter left $300 to Malden toward the bell, cast by Paul Revere,[75] that hung in its turret.[76] A clock made by the master Roxbury clockmaker Simon Willard was presented by John Harris of Charlestown. The town government rented the hall from the congregation for $45 annually. Town meetings and voters gathered here. Public meetings, lectures and traveling shows were booked here. The nascent literary organization in the town, the Malden Lyceum, also held its meetings here.[77]

Perhaps the most colorful character to come out of Malden, the eccentric "Lord" Timothy Dexter, was born "when grat powers Rouled," in 1747.[78] He was apprenticed to a farmer in Malden for six years and then to a leather-dresser in Charlestown. Freed from his apprenticeship, Dexter moved to Newburyport. There he made his fortune investing in heavily depreciated colonial currency. Once the new federal government moved to back these bills, their value increased threefold and Dexter instantly amassed a fortune.[79] He hired Jonathan Plummer to serve as his personal poet laureate to write verse about him.[80] Dexter built an elaborate mansion on High Street in Newburyport decorated with dozens of wooden statues of presidents, statesmen, kings and philosophers for everyone to see. He called it his museum.[81] He even staged his own mock funeral.[82] His book, *A Pickle for the Knowing Ones*, contained no punctuation and atrocious spelling; the second edition provided two pages of punctuation marks, inviting the

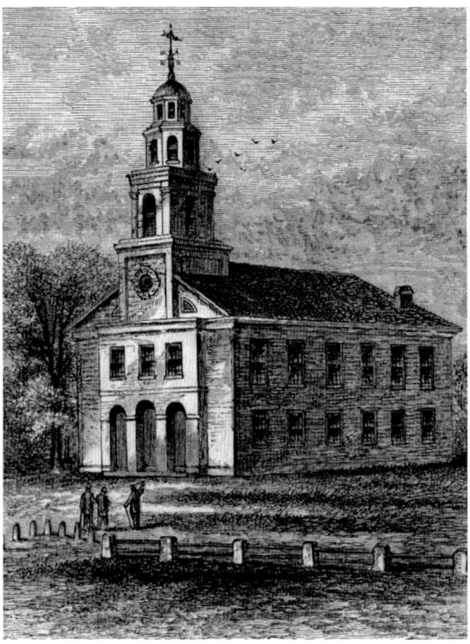

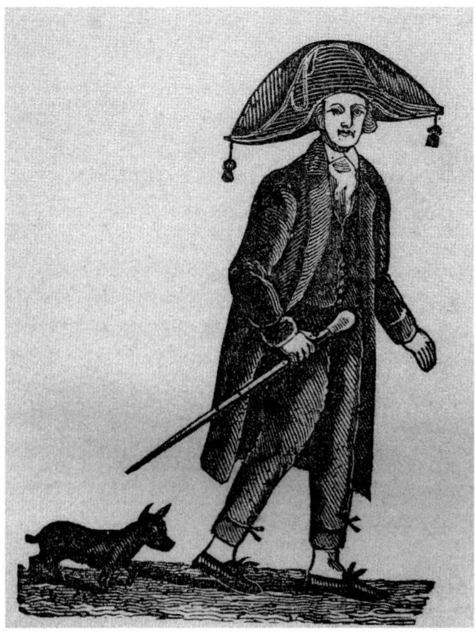

Left: The First Parish was erected in 1802 on Main Street; the site was opposite Sacred Hearts Church. *Malden Historical Society.*

Right: The eccentric "Lord" Timothy Dexter was born in Malden in 1747, moved to Newburyport and amassed a fortune. *Malden Historical Society.*

reader to "peper and solt it as they please."[83] At his death in 1806, Dexter also left $2,000 in trust to the Town of Malden to be held at interest for one hundred years and the interest to be used annually "for the support of the gospel" in Malden.[84]

The Malden church would not stay unified for long in its new meetinghouse. After Baptists and the Methodists withdrew from the church, a theological rift arose as some members harbored a growing belief in universal salvation (Universalists). Compounding this rift, Baptists and Methodists could continue to vote on Malden church matters, often not in the interests of the Malden church. At the annual parish meeting to choose a pastor in 1828, the Universalists held a majority over the traditional Congregationalists and called Sylvanus Cobb as the minister. The Congregationalists left the church and held services elsewhere. They claimed to be the old church in teaching, although the Universalists remained in the possession of the meetinghouse, parsonage, church silver and church funds. Several years of litigation ensued, with the ultimate result that the Universalists retained the church property and funds.[85] The Congregationalists organized in 1832 in the name of the Trinitarian Congregational Society, which later became the First Church in Malden, Congregational. After this split of the Malden church, church affairs became less entwined with the town government. Indeed, by amendment to the state's constitution, Massachusetts finally abolished religious taxes to support the church in 1833.[86]

Improved transportation and access to Malden was also demanded by a growing population. On September 28, 1787, what was then a marvel of modern engineering, the Malden Bridge, was completed. Spanning the Mystic River between Charlestown and South Malden—now Everett—the Malden Bridge was a second land route from Boston to points north, replacing the Penny Ferry, which had been located at the same spot. Previously, the only land route to Malden from Boston was through Medford over the Cradock Bridge. The opening of the Malden Bridge tore at the heart of Medford commerce, and Medford did not take the loss lightly.[87] That opponent of change, Dr. David Osgood, wrote of Malden's plans: "I have been so agitated about the execrable bridge at Penny Ferry, that law and divinity have both been obliged to stand by whilst I have rallied all my powers to fight the bridge-builders. And still the combat is not over. The people are bridge-mad." Osgood blamed officials in Charlestown. He wrote, "For them so immediately to turn upon us, and appear so zealous for the destruction of Medford, is a conduct so base and ungenerous as

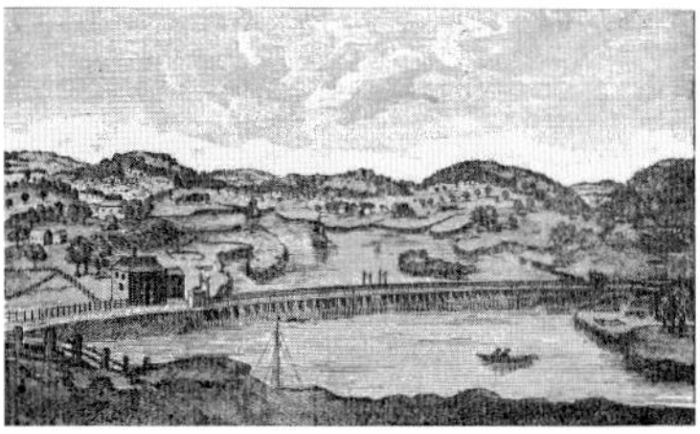

View of the Malden Bridge, which opened in 1787 across the Mystic River at the site of the Penny Ferry. Charlestown is to the left, and the Malden shore (now Everett) is to the right. *Malden Historical Society*.

nothing can palliate." Nor did Osgood mince words for those whom he termed "the Malden miserables":

> *They were never awake till the talk about this bridge put them in motion, like men who walk in their sleep. They now leave their corn unhoed, and their grass not cut, to carry petitions to court for a bridge…the distracted creatures think that if there should be a bridge, they shall at once commence a seaport town, have still-houses, stores, and what-not. And in consequence of this wretched delusion, and that neglect of business among them which it occasions, their families next winter will have no bread, and their cattle no hay.*[88]

Osgood's outrage failed to deter Malden and Charlestown, and the bridge was built. Adding insult to injury, unknowingly when George Washington, on a tour of New England, rode out from Boston to visit his Medford friend Major General John Brooks in 1789, he rode over the Malden Bridge.[89]

The completion of the Malden Bridge is credited with "opening up" the North Shore to those seeking summer diversion, not necessarily to the delight of North Shore natives.[90] The bridge's opening on September 29, 1787, ameliorated the desperate condition of the town. Malden now had a direct route to Boston and Charlestown, whereas before travelers made a circuitous route through Medford or passed through Chelsea on the way to Penny Ferry. The bridge was built with private capital and for the next seventy-two years was operated as a toll bridge by the Malden Bridge Corporation. Although it served an acute need, the tolls on the bridge constituted a heavy burden for many.[91] When a proposal was raised for a third bridge across the Mystic River, situated between the Malden and Chelsea bridges, the bridge owners circulated a pamphlet criticizing this proposed new bridge as impinging on their toll income and bringing "ruin" to their bridges.[92] Tolls were not eliminated on the Malden Bridge until 1859.

With the opening of the Malden Bridge, roadbuilding in the town continued apace. In 1796, a county road was laid out from Main Street to Black Ann's Corner in Linden.[93] In 1803, the legislature authorized the construction of the Newburyport Turnpike,[94] and in 1805–6, this "straight road" was completed to connect with the Malden Bridge.[95] Soon thereafter, the Eastern Stage Company established a passenger and mail stage run from Newburyport to Boston.[96]

With the opening of the Malden Bridge and the Newburyport Turnpike, Malden began to see growth, both in population and in industry.[97] The largest and most prosperous of these new industries was Barrett's Dye House. William Barrett was a younger son of a prominent Concord, Massachusetts family. Apprenticed to a local clothier, he learned the dyeing business and eventually went into partnership in Charlestown with an experienced English dyer. The business dyed cloth, garments and household furnishings of all types for merchants and for households. In 1803, Barrett, who was now running the business on his own, purchased land in Malden, setting up a silk dyeing business using the water and water power from Spot Pond Brook. The operations were located on the site of the parking lot behind today's post office on Mountain Avenue, which was then called Mill Street. He later entered into partnership with Meshack Shattuck.[98] The firm conducted

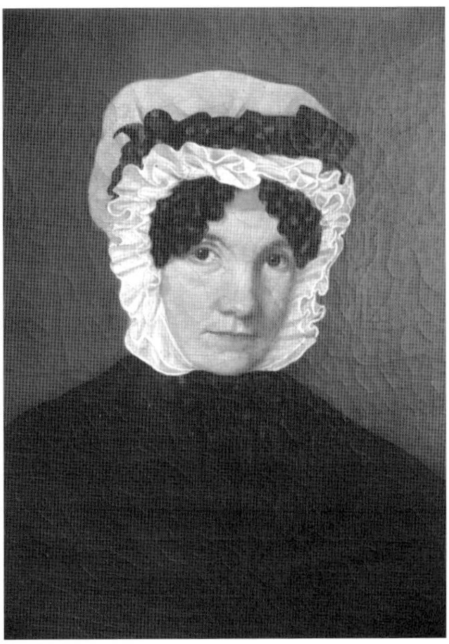

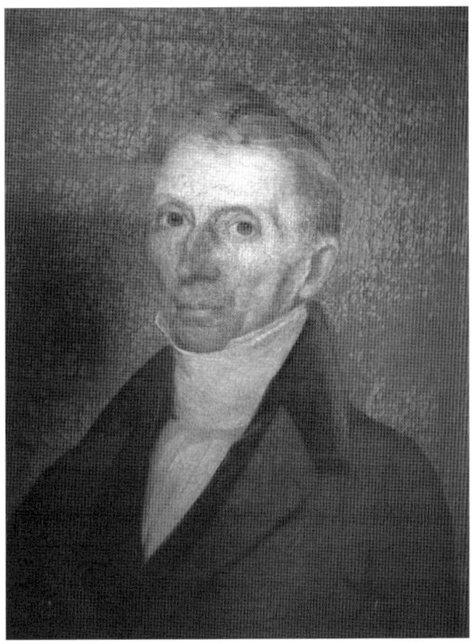

Left: Mary Kaiser Hall Barrett (1783–1840). *Right*: William Barrett (1775–1834), by Francis Alexander (1833). *Porter-Phelps-Huntington Museum/photo by Douglas Heath and Alison Simcox.*

business under the name Barrett & Shattuck until Shattuck's death in 1811. The business maintained an office in Boston and developed a network of agents in other cities such as Salem, Providence, Portsmouth, Hartford and Newport. Barrett also ran a mill upstream closer to Spot Pond (the "Red Mill") that processed dyewoods and other dyestuffs. Barrett's wooden factory burned to the ground in 1816; undeterred, he promptly replaced it with a brick dye house. In 1820, a second Barrett factory opened on Staten Island, New York.

In 1849, it was remarked that Barrett had done more to advance the business interests of the town than any previous Malden resident.[99] That Barrett was wealthy and of means is without doubt. We know he and his wife, Mary, had at least one indentured servant, Charlotte Curtis, whom he and his family taught to "read, write, and cypher," as well as "sew, knit, spin and to do all other branches of good housekeeping."[100] Barrett's son, Henry, built a large mansion that still stands on Concord Street.

Malden's other large industry was operated by the Odiorne family. In 1806, the three Odiorne brothers—George, Thomas and Ebenezer—purchased Spot Pond and the water rights to Spot Pond Brook, which had been originally granted to Thomas Coytemore, where they established a nail-rolling mill on the site of Coytemore's old gristmill in 1806.[101] The Odiornes purchased a patent from Jesse Reed, who had invented a

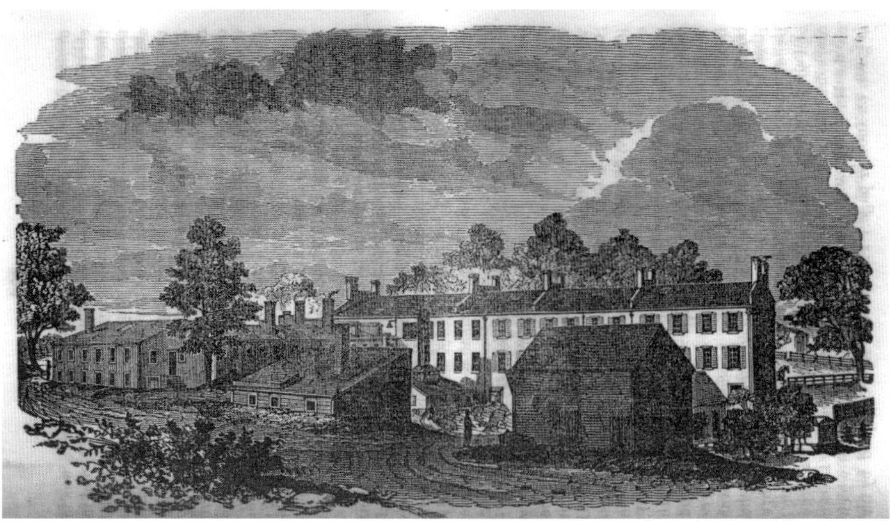

Barrett's Dye House was built in 1816 by William Barrett to replace his 1803 mill, which burned. *Malden Historical Society*.

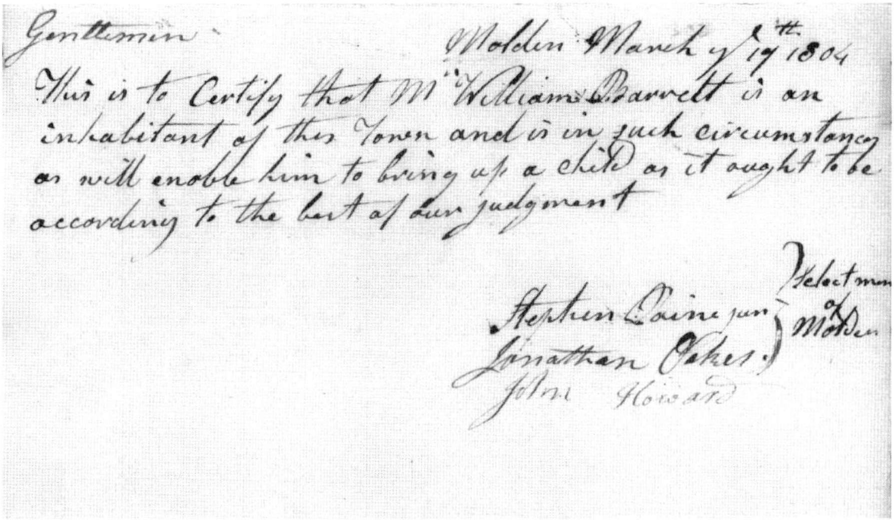

Gentlemen: Malden March y^e 19th 1804

This is to Certify that Mr William Barrett is an inhabitant of this Town and is in such circumstances as will enable him to bring up a child as it ought to be according to the best of our judgment

Stephen Paine jun } Selectmen
Jonathan Oakes } of
John Howard } Malden

The Malden selectmen certify that William Barrett is suitable to raise indentured servant Charlotte Curtis. *Boston Public Library.*

nail-cutting machine. By 1809, twenty-two of the Reed machines were operating in Odiorne's factory in Malden.[102] In 1810, the Odiornes incorporated under the name of the Malden Nail Manufactory.[103] The Odiornes perfected the first system to cut and head nails in the same operation, thus enabling them to produce nails quicker and at less cost than English nails.[104] Previously, making nails had largely been a household chore done with a small forge in a chimney corner.[105] While the nails were manufactured in Malden, the Odiornes maintained a nail store in Boston.[106] They also operated two mill seats in Pennsylvania, one outside Philadelphia at Rockdale.[107] Men and young boys were employed in their factories.[108] The Odiornes' nail cutting and heading machine came into extensive use in America and in England.[109] The brothers displayed their wealth in the opulent Greek Revival home that they built on Cedar Street. Thomas Odiorne had first tried his hand at writing and published *The Progress of Refinement* in 1792.[110] It explores man's relationship with nature, an early American expression of the Romantic movement in literature. Brickmaking was also a large trade in Malden after 1800.[111] Barrett and the Odiornes were instrumental in altering the agrarian nature of Malden. By 1820, the United States Census recorded that 257 persons in Malden were engaged in manufactures, while 172 persons were employed in agriculture.[112]

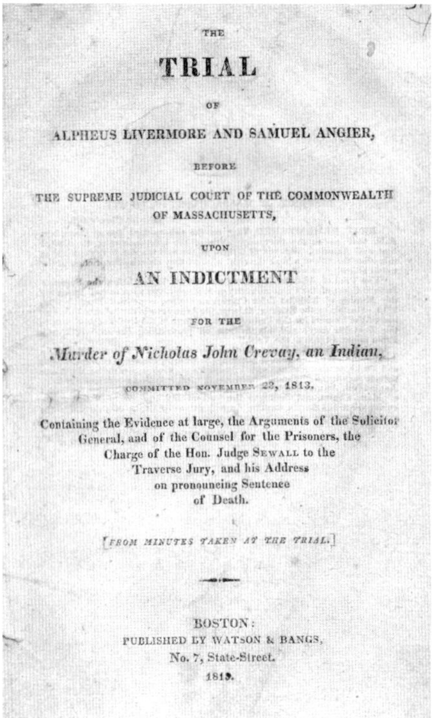

THE

TRIAL

OF

ALPHEUS LIVERMORE AND SAMUEL ANGIER,

BEFORE

THE SUPREME JUDICIAL COURT OF THE COMMONWEALTH OF MASSACHUSETTS,

UPON

AN INDICTMENT

FOR THE

Murder of Nicholas John Crevay, an Indian,

COMMITTED NOVEMBER 22, 1813.

Containing the Evidence at large, the Arguments of the Solicitor General, and of the Counsel for the Prisoners, the Charge of the Hon. Judge SEWALL to the Traverse Jury, and his Address on pronouncing Sentence of Death.

[*FROM MINUTES TAKEN AT THE TRIAL.*]

BOSTON:
PUBLISHED BY WATSON & BANGS,
No. 7, State-Street.
181[illegible].

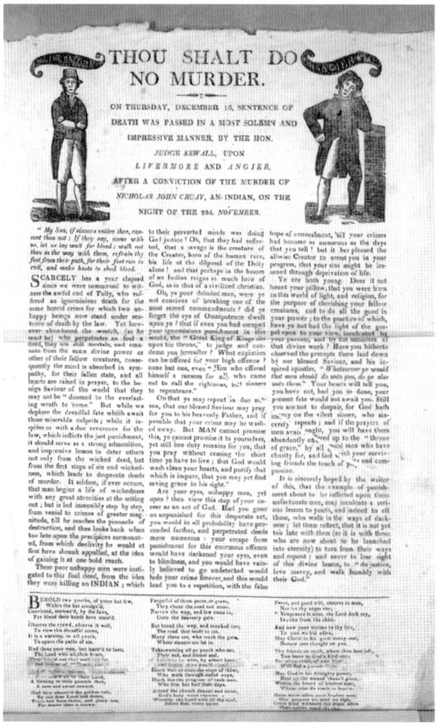

THOU SHALT DO NO MURDER.

ON THURSDAY, DECEMBER 15, SENTENCE OF DEATH WAS PASSED IN A MOST SOLEMN AND IMPRESSIVE MANNER, BY THE HON. *JUDGE SEWALL*, UPON *LIVERMORE* AND *ANGIER*, AFTER A CONVICTION OF THE MURDER OF *NICHOLAS JOHN CRUAY*, AN INDIAN, ON THE NIGHT OF THE 22d. *NOVEMBER*.

"*My Son, if sinners entice thee, consent thou not: If they say, come with us, let us lay wait for blood; walk not thou in the way with them, refrain thy foot from their path, for their feet run to evil, and make haste to shed blood.*"

Left: Front cover of the report of the trial of Alpheus Livermore and Samuel Angier for the brutal murder of Indian Nicholas Crevay at Spot Pond. *Author's collection.*

Right: One of two broadsides that were rushed into print about the trial of Livermore and Angier. *American Antiquarian Society.*

A tragic murder and noteworthy trial are associated with the Odiorne family. In November 1813, four nailworkers—Samuel Angier, Alpheus Livermore, Mark Packard and John Winch—set off from the Odiorne manufactory with guns loaded with Odiorne nails intending to "rout" an Indian couple encamped on the shores of Spot Pond.[113] According to the trial report, the husband, Nicholas Crevay, had been intoxicated and acting "saucy" and improper in Malden.[114] There was also some resentment, as Crevay had beat some nailworkers in wrestling matches on the shores of the Spot Pond.[115] Perhaps another motive was that the Indians were squatting on Odiorne property. Nicholas Crevay was murdered and his wife, Sally, seriously wounded.

Because of the atrocity of the murder, the case attracted attention in the Boston press.[116] Mark Packard fled to Rockdale, where he continued to work for the Odiornes. Alpheus Livermore and Samuel Angier were tried before the Supreme Judicial Court for the murder of Crevay, found guilty and sentenced to hang. Livermore was the son of Jason Livermore, pastor of the Baptist church. The fourth participant in the crime, John Winch, was tried separately and acquitted. Two broadsides and an account of the trial were rushed into print.[117] Despite their convictions, numerous petitions for clemency were filed with the Governor's Council, one signed by four selectmen of Malden. Assisted by the Odiornes, a committee set out to gather additional evidence. It was the largest petition campaign Massachusetts had ever seen.[118]

After consideration, the committee determined that there was reason to believe Angier and Livermore did not intend to kill Crevay but that they knew or should have known the guns were loaded with nails and therefore were guilty "in a legal if not a moral sense."[119] The committee recommended, and the governor and council adopted, a recommendation of life in prison. After an additional round of petitions, again joined in by the Malden selectmen, and after serving just over four years in prison, Livermore and Angier were released.[120] As historian Richard Brown wrote, "Massachusetts' long record of not executing a white for murdering an Indian would persist."[121] Indeed, that belief, based on this trial, would spread among Indians, at least in New England.[122] Nicholas Crevay and Sally were interred in Stoneham's burial ground. As a final affront, their bodies were stolen, either an act of desecration or, as was sometimes the practice, to be used for dissection in a medical school.[123]

In addition to Barrett's dye works and the Odiorne nail factory, other industries also flourished in Malden. Timothy Bailey and James H. Putnam operated a tin factory that turned out block-tin, tinplate and pewter articles under the name Bailey & Putnam.[124] Putnam later went out on his own, opening a shop across the street from Bailey. The factory was located near the south corner of Main and Madison Streets and employed eight workmen. Bailey also employed sixteen salesmen and wagons to distribute his finished products to Malden and the surrounding areas.[125] The Cox Last Company, Baldwin's dye house and Jonathan Robinson's rolling mill were other early industries. The southern part of the town also appears to have benefited from fishing and clamming.[126] Frederick Tudor, the "ice king," harvested ice on Swain's Pond and Spot Pond.[127] By its 200th anniversary, Malden could count among its industries the rolling and nail mill, three dye houses, seven forges and businesses producing cutlery, pewter, carriages, boots, shoes and leather.

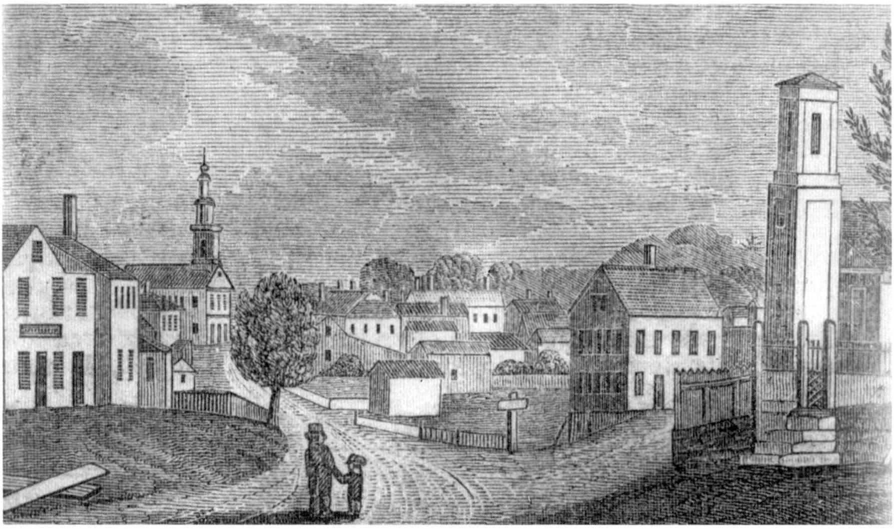

Malden Center in 1837 is seen in this woodcut. The view is from the intersection of Main, Madison and Eastern Avenue, looking north up Main Street. *Malden Historical Society.*

Increased industry created a demand for a local bank to provide not only a place of safekeeping but also a source of financing. In 1833, Timothy Bailey established the Malden Agricultural and Mechanics Association, which in 1851 became the First National Bank of Malden.[128]

Commercial growth increased the value of building lots in Malden Center, as the junction of the Medford (Pleasant Street) and Reading (Main Street) Roads became a profitable place to locate a business. It sometimes resulted in litigation, as in 1835, when John Sprague removed an old stone wall and built a fence into the traveled path of the Medford Road, about where Pleasant Street intersects Main Street. Darius Waite, a town surveyor, removed the obstruction. Sprague sued Waite for trespass. Waite ultimately prevailed, but this innocuous case provided a description of Malden Center in 1835.[129] At the time, Main Street was called Reading Road, and Pleasant Street was called Medford Road. The Spot Pond Brook crossed under a bridge in the Medford Road just west of the intersection. Part of the traveled way passed directly through the brook and was used as a watering hole. A stone wall ran along the Reading Road and followed the curve of the Medford Road, ending at the bridge.

That the increased population and number of dwellings and industries required protection is evident from the development of a fire department in Malden as early as 1820. Malden had a band of volunteer firefighters and purchased a primitive engine called the "Alert." In 1833, a company of fifty men composed the volunteer fire department, and their firehouse was on the corner of Pleasant and Middlesex Streets. They were compensated by an abatement of their poll taxes. By 1839, the legislature had formally created a fire department in Malden.[130] Engines were purchased for other parts of the town: the "Endeavor" for North Malden and the "General Taylor" for South Malden. The "Daniel Webster" was purchased to protect Edgeworth in 1854. The first steam fire engine, the "Wannalancet," was added a decade later.

Chapter 5

THE RAILROAD, INDUSTRY AND IMMIGRATION

Malden's growth had barely begun when the coming of the Boston & Maine Railroad in 1845 sowed the seeds for more rapid growth in population, industry and land speculation over the next forty years. Malden was served by the western division of the Boston & Maine Railroad, and in 1853, it was joined by the Saugus Branch Railroad. There were three stops on the western division[131] and six stations on the Saugus Branch.[132] The railroad brought Malden within easy access of Boston and lured land speculators and "money-getting" men to Malden: "It is now beginning to be known that the face of the country in Malden is diversified with various attractions of land and water scenery. Here, within five miles of Boston, are woody heights and rocky glens, and smooth rounded hills, clothed in the summer's livery of green; and affording numerous prospects combining the charms of city, sea, and country. The prospect from 'Wait's Mountain' on a clear day is a vision of beauty. Lovers, poets, and money-getting matter-of-fact men, all assert this with equal enthusiasm."[133]

In the 1840s, Malden was still very much a rural place, sparsely settled and not built up. This was largely due to the high tolls on the Malden Bridge, a bridge that had initially been a boon to the town. However, the construction of another toll bridge over the Mystic River at Chelsea and the opening of the Salem Turnpike had taken most of the north–south travel away from Malden. Without this traffic passing through, Malden had fallen into an economic slump. In 1849, it was noted that Malden, "cut off from Boston by two toll bridges...had flourished less than some

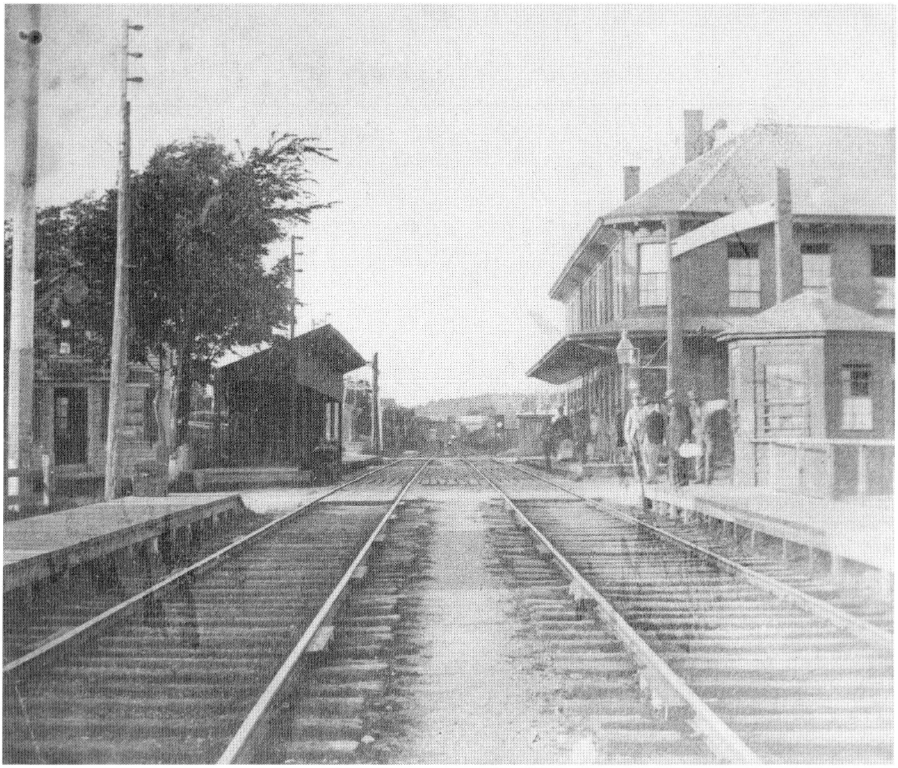

Malden's first railroad station. The arrival of the railroad in 1845 spurred development in Malden and the separation of Melrose from Malden in 1850. *Malden Historical Society.*

more favored towns in the environs of the great city."[134] With the advent of the railroad, this would soon change.

One of the earliest land speculation enterprises that realized the relative value of Malden real estate was the Edgeworth Company, incorporated in 1849.[135] The Edgeworth Company purchased the Newton farm, which sat on the west bank of the Malden River and encompassed most of Edgeworth. Its sister company, the Malden Highlands Company, purchased a tract of land in the highlands north of Pleasant Street. The companies drew plans, laid out lots and offered inducements to prospective purchasers. One-sixth of the Edgeworth Company's land had been sold by the town's 200th anniversary in 1849.[136] On this land, the neighborhood now called Edgeworth was developed, and several large manufacturing plants located there, namely the Boston Rubber Shoe Company and Cochrane Chemical Works. By 1857, the Malden Highlands Company was advertising land in the western part of Malden, north of Pleasant Street and west of Highland Avenue. As land speculation grew, old place names were discarded in favor of names deemed more picturesque and, thus, saleable: Tyot became Oak Grove, Scadan became Maplewood, and the Medford Road was renamed Pleasant Street.

In 1849, Malden celebrated its 200th anniversary in grand style. The town held a large gathering at Bell Rock with an oration and a banquet under a tent. There was a general illumination, with lanterns hung in windows and across the streets, and a bonfire on a float in the pond in Malden Center. Townspeople enjoyed fireworks and listened to music of the Brigade and Salem bands.[137]

As with the railroad, speculators sought to improve water access to Malden as well. In 1846, the Malden Canal Company was chartered with the purpose of dredging and straightening the Malden River.[138] The river was straightened for commerce, and by the 1850s, Otis Tufts had erected the first wharf near the historic landing place at Sandy Bank. The once curvy river, straightened and no longer recognizable, was soon home to barges and ships carrying coal, tar and other products to and from local manufacturers.

In 1850, a small factory would open in Malden that, unknown to those at the time, would prove to become the predecessor to Malden's most successful and lucrative industry. The Edgeworth Rubber Company constructed a factory at Edgeworth, intent on competing with four larger companies operating under licenses from Charles Goodyear.[139] The Edgeworth Rubber Company failed, and its assets, including the real estate, were sold to the Malden Manufacturing Company in 1853. In September 1853, a young businessman, Elisha S. Converse, won election as the treasurer of the Malden Manufacturing Company, which promptly changed its name to the Boston Rubber Shoe Company. Converse would hold this position for forty-one years.

The principals of the Boston Rubber Shoe Company were all investors or businessmen: Gardiner Greene Hubbard; William Judson, legal counsel to Charles Goodyear; T.C. Wales, rubber shoe businessman; John Bertram, Salem merchant and rubber importer; Joshua Sylvester; and Nathaniel Hayward.[140] Hayward, although less well known than Goodyear, made pioneering discoveries in the development of crude rubber vulcanizing.[141]

Hubbard played an integral role in Malden's development. A Cambridge attorney and large land speculator in Greater Boston, he was the force behind the Edgeworth Company and Malden Highlands Company. Hubbard, along with Converse, was one of the incorporators of the Malden Bank

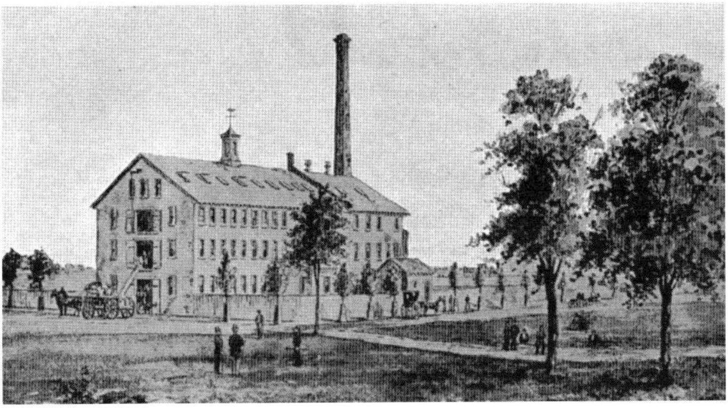

The first wooden factory of the Boston Rubber Shoe Company in Edgeworth, seen in 1853. *Malden Historical Society.*

in 1851. Hubbard later went on to found the National Geographic Society and was president of Bell Telephone Company. His daughter, Mabel, married Alexander Graham Bell. Converse stayed in touch with Hubbard through the years and was an early investor in the Bell telephone; he also met Alexander Graham Bell.[142]

Born in Needham in 1820, Elisha Converse would become Malden's great philanthropist and benefactor. At the age of four, Converse and his family moved to Thompson, Connecticut. After attending school in Boston, Converse returned to Thompson and went into business as a clothier. Converse married Mary Diana Edmands in 1843. In 1844, Converse returned to Boston and partnered with Benjamin Poland in the wholesale of boots and shoes. By 1847, the Converses had moved to Haywardville in Stoneham to the "Red Mills," where Poland and Converse had a business grinding and preparing drugs, spices and dyes. The Converse & Poland concern dissolved in 1849. The same year, Converse partnered with John Robson as Converse & Robson and continued to conduct the grinding and preparation business in the same mill, the partnership lasting until 1853.

Hubbard enticed Converse to relocate his business from Haywardville to Malden.[143] By 1855, the Boston Rubber Shoe Company was producing four hundred pairs of shoes per day.[144] In 1868, its wooden factory was moved and a new brick mill built at Edgeworth.[145] By 1871, the roles of treasurer and superintendent were combined, and Converse became, in effect, the manager of the entire operation of the company.[146] He was elected president of the company in 1894.[147]

Converse took a paternalistic interest in his employees, which included children. In 1873, a free library was organized at the factory for the benefit of the employees. That same year, a Relief Society began to aid those

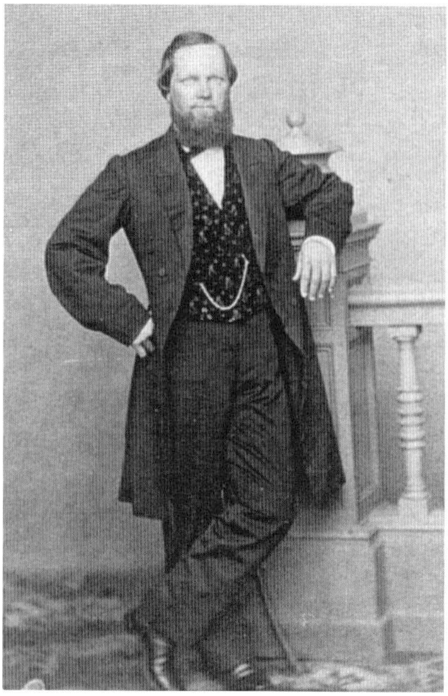

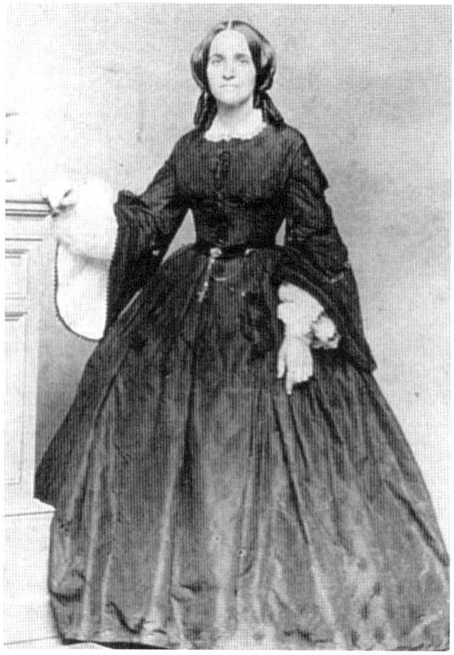

employees who were sick or were injured while working in the factory. In November 1875, a fire destroyed both the old wooden factory and the brick factory, throwing 800 employees out of work and killing a thirteen-year-old boy. By May 1876, a new four-story brick factory was operating at Edgeworth, producing fifteen thousand pairs of shoes per day.[148] The Edgeworth factory grew, employing more than 1,500 workers and producing twenty thousand pairs of shoes per day.[149] The company maintained an office and five-story warehouse on Causeway Street in Boston. In 1881, a second factory was built in Melrose, near Oak Grove. Comprising five acres of floor space and employing more than 1,000 people, it produced twelve thousand pairs of shoes per day.[150] The company was noted for its "storm slipper" (a rubber overshoe) and for its line of rubber boots.[151] By 1898, it had succumbed to the rubber trust and became a unit of the United States Rubber Company.[152]

In 1850, the Converses moved to Linden Avenue in Malden and, by 1859, had begun building their magnificent residence on Main Street on an expansive plot of land bounded by Perkins Avenue, Wyllis Avenue and Bell Rock Street. Henry Cabot Lodge came to tea and commented that the Converse home "showed plenty of money and generous expenditure but everything tasteless."[153] Most Malden residents likely did not agree.

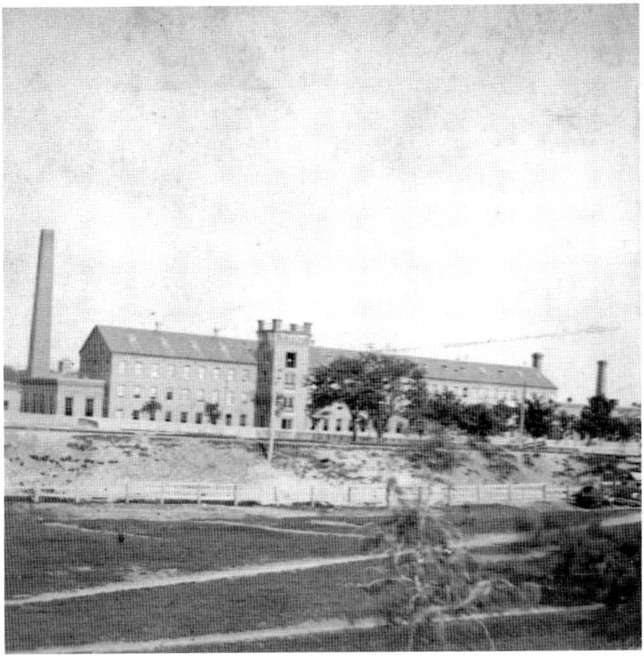

Left: The first brick factory of the Boston Rubber Shoe Company at Edgeworth was built in 1868. *Malden Historical Society*.

Opposite, left: Elisha Slade Converse is seen in this rare photograph, probably from around 1850. *Malden Historical Society*.

Opposite, right: Mary Diana Converse, seen in an early photograph, circa 1850. *Malden Historical Society*.

Converse by and large used his wealth for Malden's benefit. He also lived for a time in Boston, maintaining the Malden home and a Boston address. He lived at the Hotel Vendome and 1 Gloucester Street for a time before acquiring a Back Bay townhouse at 348 Beacon Street. Converse and his older brother, James, were deacons in the Baptist church and often used the appellation "Deacon" before their names. For many years, Elisha Converse served on the Malden water board. He was director and president of Malden's First National Bank from his election in 1856 for forty-nine years.

Local citizens elected Converse as their state representative in 1879–80 and as state senator in 1880–81.[154] While in the legislature, he secured a city charter for Malden and was elected, almost unanimously, as the city's first mayor. He ran for the Republican nomination for Congress in 1882 in the then Sixth District. After a bitter campaign, Converse beat out Henry Cabot Lodge for the party's nomination after 130 ballots. Lodge had a poor opinion of Converse but campaigned for him in the general election. The campaign ended in defeat with a Democratic victory.[155] At Malden's 250th anniversary, Converse penned a response to a toast: "Though this was not my birthplace, Malden has been the home of my life, and it is endeared to me by many sad and many happy memories. In the midst of

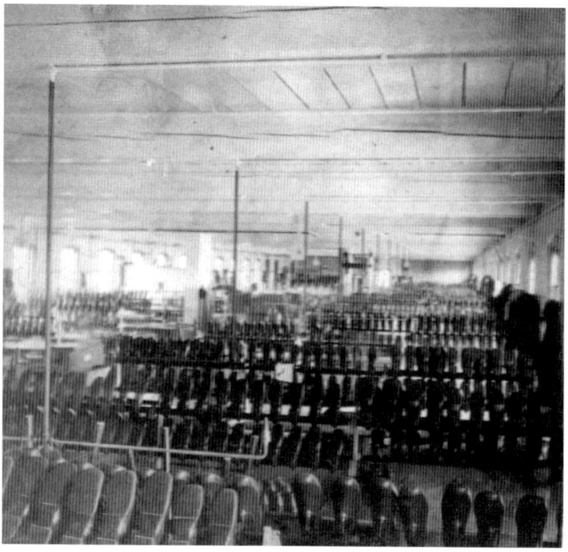

The boot room of the Boston Rubber Shoe Company gives an idea of the volume of the factory's production. *Malden Historical Society*.

her people I have met all the varied joys and sorrows which come to the life of man. In the many friendships which have come to me here I have found inspiration and strength. I feel all the loyalty to the good old town that a native can feel."[156]

Converse's philanthropic endeavors were legion. He donated the Converse Memorial Building of the Malden Public Library, Pine Banks Park, land for the Malden Hospital and a memorial tablet in Converse Hall in the Tremont Temple Baptist Church in Boston.[157] He gave the people of Malden use of the reservoir when Fellsmere Park was developed. He contributed liberally to the erection of the First Baptist Church, the Malden YMCA, the Malden Auditorium and the Malden Home for the Aged.[158] He was, at various times, trustee of Wellesley College and a member of the Trustees of Reservations, as well as active in the preservation of the Middlesex Fells. He either founded or participated in the Malden Industrial Aid Society, the Malden Improvement Association, the Malden Historical Society and the Malden Civil Service Reform Association. Converse died in 1904 and is buried at Woodlawn Cemetery.

The Potter Drug and Chemical Company arrived in Malden in 1892, ushering in the beginning of what was to become one of Malden's best-known products: Cuticura soaps.[159] Frederick Robinson founded Robinson Bros. & Company in 1852.[160] It conducted business as the Indexical Soap Company. The company merged with Weeks & Potter, which also began in 1852. George Robert White formed Potter Drug and Chemical Company in 1883 and coined the name Cuticura.[161] By 1919, the company had consolidated production at the Malden plant, which still stands on Medford Street directly opposite the Bell Rock Cemetery.[162]

Malden's explosive growth can be seen in the population increases between the 1830s and the Civil War. From 1837, the population grew to 2,514 by 1840. In 1850, Malden's population numbered 3,520, and this did not include those residing in North Malden, which had been set off from Malden in 1850 as the new town of Melrose. By 1860, Malden's population had increased to 5,865. The burgeoning population led to the introduction of horsecars to connect Malden with Boston. The first horsecar in Malden operated on July 19, 1858; the round trip to Boston took an entire half day. The Malden and Melrose Railroad Company operated a horsecar to Haymarket Square.[163]

Newcomers to Malden did not share the same ethnic background as its earlier inhabitants. The developing factories, arrival of the railroad, ease of access to Boston and affordability of land combined to attract Irish and, near the end of the nineteenth century, Italian immigrants who worked in Malden's factories, populated its schools and leavened its social institutions.

Perhaps the earliest evidence of a growing ethnic minority can be seen in the creation of the Immaculate Conception Parish for Catholics in Malden and Medford in 1853. Before 1853, Catholics in Malden traveled long distances to attend services, usually to St. Mary's in Charlestown, it being most convenient because of the Butler coach from Malden to Boston. The round-trip fare was beyond the means of many, and the men and younger parishioners would often walk to Charlestown. The first Catholic mass in Malden was celebrated in Greene's Hall, on the corner of Pleasant and Middlesex Streets, with an original congregation numbering two hundred people. By 1855, the Immaculate Conception Church, initially called St. Mary's Church, was built, and a priest celebrated the first mass in the new church on Christmas Day.[164] That the majority of the Irish Catholics were laborers in the town's factories is evident from the remarks Reverend Richard Neagle made at a memorial service for Elisha Converse in 1904: "The greater number of the men and women, whose faithful labor contributed to his great success as a manufacturer, were, I think, of those who I am proud to call my people…and they, knowing that he was thoughtful and considerate of their welfare, repaid him with faithful service; for it is only fair to say that much of the credit for the great success of Mr. Converse in business belongs to the faithful, hard-working people of his factories."[165]

Initially, Malden's Irish Catholic population was primarily situated in Edgeworth. Immaculate Conception Parish opened a parochial school on Highland Avenue in 1881; by 1891, a school had been constructed for girls.[166] As the Catholic population grew and spread throughout Malden, additional parishes were necessary. Sacred Hearts Church was built on Main Street in 1901, along with an east side parish, later to be called St. Joseph's, in 1902. Catholic cemeteries were also established—St. Mary's in the 1850s and the expansive Holy Cross Cemetery in 1864.

To be sure, there was anti-Irish sentiment in Malden that persisted throughout the nineteenth century. Some was overt and some more subtle. As an example, shortly after successful Edgeworth grocer John J. Kelley had the temerity to build his home on Highland Avenue in the West End, a Yankee neighbor constructed his stable as close to the Kelley home as possible.[167]

German Jews had arrived in Malden as early as the 1850s, but they had no synagogue in which to worship. The Hebrew Charitable Burying Ground was established on Lebanon Street in 1851, the second Jewish cemetery in Massachusetts. It was primarily intended for indigent Jews needing a burial space near Boston.[168] Up to 1,200 children under age five were buried at the cemetery, many in unmarked graves, as families could not afford them. By the end of the nineteenth century, large numbers of Russian and Polish Jews began settling in Malden. The tide swelled after 1908 with refugees from the great Chelsea fire. The first recorded synagogue was Mishkan Tefila (Dwelling of Prayer), which met in a private home on Granville Avenue. The first synagogue erected was Agudas Achim, also known as the Harvard Street Shul, which went up in 1903 and had a congregation of 250 families.[169]

Yet not all Malden people welcomed the Jews. The author Elliott Paul, in his novelized memoir *Linden on the Saugus Branch*, alleged that the Linden Improvement Association was formed to keep property values high in the neighborhood, "which meant a thoroughgoing understanding between all property owners that neither houses nor lots would ever be sold to Jews."[170] Jewish boys were excluded from the Literary Society at Malden High School and, as a consequence, formed their own club, the Lyceum.[171]

There were African Americans in Malden but not in large numbers until the 1890s. For example, the 1800 census records nine black citizens and the 1840 census, just five.[172] In 1890, Edward A. Washington came to Malden holding religious services for black residents. Within a year, he had formed St. Luke's Baptist Church. Initially located in Bailey's Block on Pleasant Street, the church later became the Centre Street Baptist Church; then, acquiring a site on the corner of eastern Avenue and Hillside Avenue, it became the Eastern Avenue Baptist Church. A second black church was organized in 1899 as Union Baptist Church after a number of citizens met in the home of James Ivy to discuss the formation of a church. The two churches united in 1945 to form the Emmanuel Baptist Church.[173]

Although Malden has experienced rapid growth in its Asian population in the late twentieth century, Asians were virtually absent from Malden in the nineteenth century. This may be due in part to the various Chinese exclusion laws. Chinese immigration was first authorized by the Burlingame Treaty in 1868 but was largely suspended by 1882 with the Chinese Exclusion Act.[174] A notable exception was Oong ArShowe, who was born in 1824 in China and immigrated to Malden before 1868. Taking the American name Charles ArShowe, he operated a tea store on Union Street in Boston. ArShowe's advertisement in the 1865 Boston directory is the earliest evidence of a Chinese business in Boston.[175] He became a member of Mount Vernon Lodge of Masons and erected a home on Waite Street in Maplewood.

With the growth of the population, social organizations flourished. The Malden Lyceum—a literary society of the town that sponsored lectures in the meetinghouse and, later, the town hall—was founded in about 1835.[176] In 1860, the Lyceum attracted three well-known speakers to Malden: Charles Sumner, Wendell Phillips and Edward Everett Hale.[177] The Malden Temperance Society was organized in about 1830.[178] A military company called the Washington Guards was formed. Annual musters on the plains between Malden and Medford were a source of entertainment,[179] as were winter sleigh races on Pleasant Street and Salem Street between Medford and Malden squares.[180] These races inspired Medford's James Pierpont to write "Jingle Bells."[181] Mount Vernon Lodge of Masons began in 1857. A newspaper, the *Malden Messenger*, began publishing in 1856. Before that, locals received news through the Boston papers or the *Bunker Hill Aurora*. Other papers soon followed.[182]

Townspeople created a short-lived subscription library in the first quarter of the nineteenth century. In 1853, the Malden Lyceum began a private subscription library and fitted up rooms in the Waite Block. This, too, was short-lived. In 1857, the Malden Agricultural Library was instituted, but it fared no better than its predecessors.[183] It would be another twenty years before Malden established a library that lasted.

The town had outgrown the fourth meetinghouse and, in 1856, voted to build a new town house. Purchasing the Hills Tavern land on Main

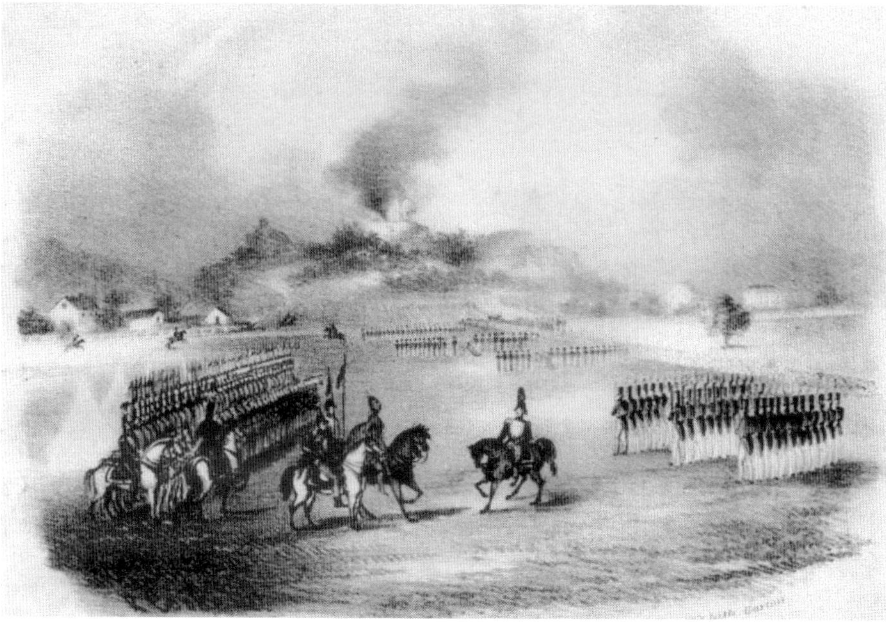

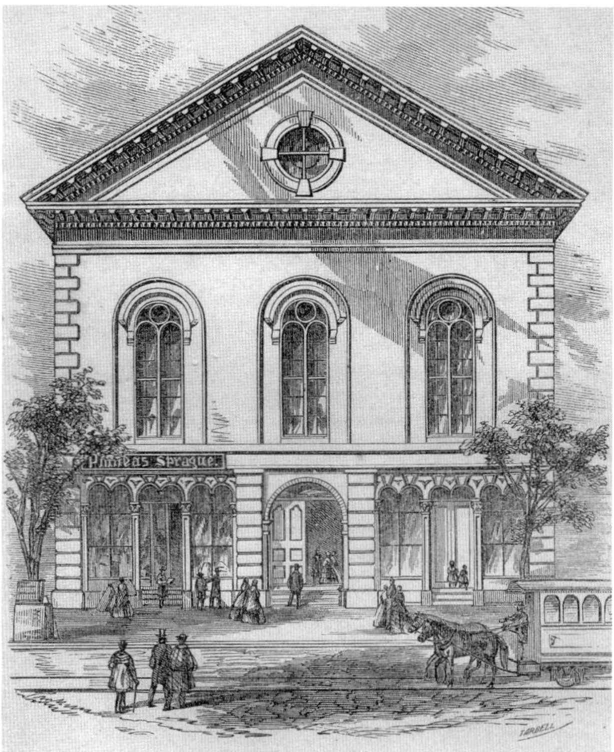

Above: Engraving of the Indian muster, a sham fight between soldiers and "Indians," on the plains of Edgeworth in 1838. The Medford Road (Pleasant Street) runs from left to right in the rear. *Malden Historical Society*.

Left: The town house (old city hall) built on Main Street opposite Pleasant Street in 1857 on the site of Hill's Tavern. *Malden Historical Society*.

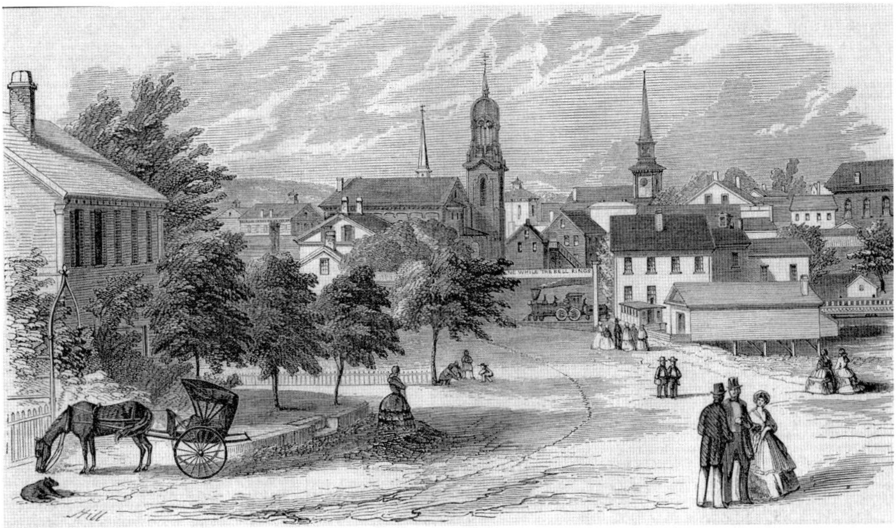

Malden Center as seen in 1858. The view is looking north up Main Street from the intersection of Madison Street and Eastern Avenue. *From left to right*: the steeples of the Methodist Church, First Parish and Congregational Church. The town house is at right. *Author's collection.*

Street, the town moved the tavern south to the corner of Irving Street and built a brick town house. Jonathan Clark constructed it. Clark built his own house at 35 Wyoming Avenue. The town house was dedicated on October 29, 1857, with Gilbert Haven, the younger, presiding; the united choirs of the town rejoiced, "Joy! Joy! Freedom today!"[184] Soon after the opening, Phineas Sprague moved his dry goods store to the ground floor—convenient for him since his office as town treasurer was in the rear of the building. A large hall on the second floor was used for town meetings and was rented out to various organizations. The police department maintained a lockup in the basement.

The town also outgrew the space at the old burying ground at Bell Rock. The town purchased a lot to the rear of the old Baptist meetinghouse on Salem Street in 1832 known as the new burying ground. With additions of land in the 1860s, this became the Salem Street Cemetery.[185] Wealthier residents of Malden and Boston organized a private cemetery, Woodlawn, in 1850, which when it opened was located in Malden and Chelsea—today this area is now part of Everett and Revere. Woodlawn was the third rural cemetery in Greater Boston. It was designed as a garden cemetery following in the nature of Mount Auburn Cemetery in Cambridge.[186]

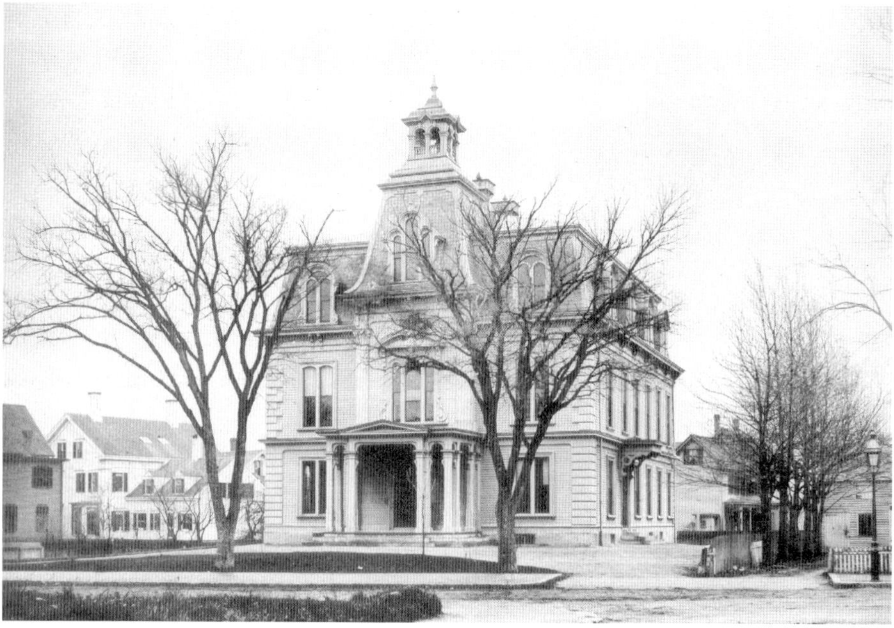

The first wooden high school building on Salem Street was built in 1872. *Malden Historical Society.*

Massachusetts adopted a compulsory high school law in 1827 that mandated towns to set up high schools. The law, however, was loosely enforced until 1837, when Horace Mann became education commissioner.[187] Nonetheless, it took Malden until 1857 to vote that the school committee should establish a high school. A room was fitted up in the Centre Grammar School, then located on Pleasant Street. The high school opened with thirty-eight students and increased during the year to fifty-three.[188] By 1859, the high school had outgrown its quarters and moved into two rooms on the south side of the town house, where it remained until a separate high school building was erected in 1872. The high school was originally an exam school, with applicants required to take an admission test. This was soon abolished.

The school also developed social institutions that prepared students for entrance into Malden society. In 1872, for example, four boys, fresh from discussing the heated elections of 1872, decided to form a society, and the idea "fell like a spark into a keg of powder."[189] Thus, the Malden High School Literary Society ("Lit") was founded, and it remains today the oldest continuous public high school club in the nation. Lit began the first school newspaper, *The Oracle*, in 1888.[190] In the school's early days, military drill was popular, and membership in the high school battalion was sought after. By the later nineteenth century, interest in military drill had waned, supplanted by athletics. In 1889, the high school established a football team, and the annual rivalry against Medford began.[191]

Chapter 6

LET US BRING SLAVERY TO ITS KNEES

Malden's Abolitionists

The Fugitive Slave Law of 1850 required all suspected fugitives to be brought before a federal commissioner, forbade testimony by the suspect and eliminated trial by jury and writ of habeas corpus. It criminalized any help rendered to an accused fugitive and encouraged the kidnapping of free blacks.[192] Abolitionists reviled the law and spurred the development of the Underground Railroad[193] There were those with antislavery sympathies in Malden. Gilbert (Senior) and Hannah Haven subscribed to antislavery newspapers.[194] James Redpath and Gilbert Haven, the younger, were noted abolitionists. David B. Morey and his wife, Almira Bailey Morey, were acquaintances of Theodore Parker, William Lloyd Garrison, Wendell Phillips and Parker Pillsbury. A small network of abolitionists in Malden assisted with the rescue of fugitive slaves by using their homes as stops on the Underground Railroad. One was at the old parsonage on Main Street, then owned by the Wilson family. The second was in the Morey House on Hillside Avenue.[195] A third station was the Haven home on Clifton Street. The fourth was the home of Redpath on Maple Street.[196] Operation of these stations was successful in no small part due to the heroism of the women who kept the homes.[197]

There were at least four petitions from Malden residents submitted annually to the General Court surrounding the Fugitive Slave Act beginning in 1858; three of these were spearheaded by David and Almira Morey. In 1858, the Moreys organized a petition to remove Judge Edward Loring.[198] The petition was signed by 30 Malden residents. In 1859, David and Almira

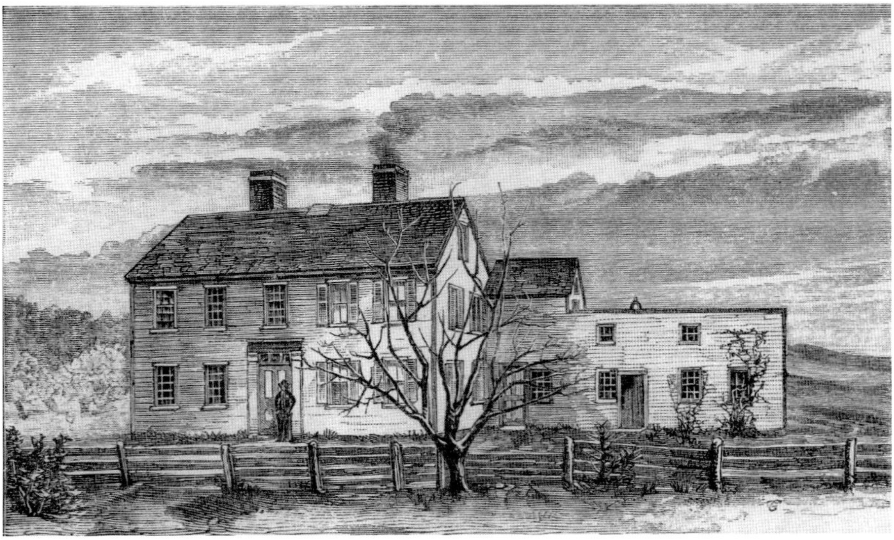

The Gilbert Haven House on Clifton Street was a stop on the Underground Railroad. *Author's collection.*

organized a petition of Malden residents against the rendition of fugitive slaves from Massachusetts that was submitted to the General Court. It was signed by 142 residents of the town. In addition to the Moreys, signatories included James Redpath and his wife, Mary; Harriet Hanson Robinson; William S. Robinson; Elisha Converse; the Cox and Haven families; and George Wilson, owner of the Parsonage. Other prominent citizens and business owners signed as well.[199] The Moreys organized a third petition in 1860 signed by 179 residents. In 1861, Nathaniel Starbird organized a petition against slave hunting signed by 57 adults of Malden, again signed by the Robinsons, Redpaths and Moreys, among others. The petitions contain many common names, and one can assume that this larger group shared a common interest in abolitionist activities in the town. To be sure, not all agreed with this position. In January 1861, Henry Barrett organized a petition to the General Court seeking the repeal of Massachusetts's personal liberty laws (i.e., those laws in conflict with the Fugitive Slave Act). It was signed by 151 voters of Malden.

David B. Morey married Almira Bailey, the daughter of Timothy Bailey. Reportedly, her father disowned her for marrying David, who was a Universalist. In 1852, the couple took up residence in Charlestown, where Morey began manufacturing pewter, specializing in lamps. He often hired ex-convicts in a belief that they could be led to a useful life.[200] Morey eventually amassed enough money to erect the house on Hillside Avenue. Friendly with activists in the abolitionist movement, the Moreys soon offered their home to shelter former slaves and even named their children after noted abolitionists.[201] Escaping slaves were hidden in the Morey basement until they could be passed along to Harriet Beecher Stowe in Andover. During a speech by Wendell Phillips at the music hall in Boston, Almira Morey was one of a phalanx of women who surrounded Phillips so he could escape the hostile crowd.[202]

When the Civil War began and the town of Malden held regular illuminations, Morey refused to illuminate his home until he knew whether the country would be slave or free. He was told by Malden officials that they could not offer him protection if he persisted. At the time of John Brown's raid, Morey and others hired Tremont Temple in Boston for an antislavery meeting despite opposition from a proslavery mob.[203] Recalling her childhood days in the Morey House, Ellen Beale Morey (also called Madam Morey) remembered, "[W]hen I used to listen in open-eyed wonder to the discussions that went on under this roof. The great thinkers of the day came to our house as a matter of course. Bronson Alcott held many conferences here. Other visitors were John M. Spear, Samuel Longfellow, David Warson, Lucretia Mott, Margaret Fuller, Lydia Maria Child, and John Weiss. They used to discuss the very subjects that are uppermost in the world's thought today—woman suffrage, peace, and temperance."[204] At David Morey's death, Parker Pillsbury gave the eulogy.[205]

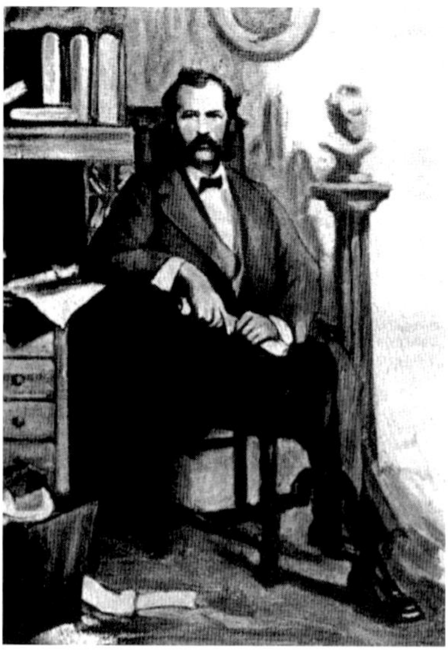

James Redpath lived on Maple Street in Malden. He was an abolitionist, journalist and friend of Mark Twain, among others. *Malden Historical Society*.

James Redpath came to Malden, which he described as "a town of rare and manifold virtues," in August 1858, settling on Maple Street.[206] Born in 1833 in Scotland, he arrived in America in 1850 and went to Michigan, where he engaged in journalism. His reports came to the attention of Horace Greeley, who lured him east as a reporter for Greeley's *New York Tribune*. He was sent to the South to report on slavery. He collected these reports in a book, *The Roving Editor*.[207]

Greely sent him to "Bleeding" Kansas to report on the debate whether Kansas would be a free or slave state.[208] Redpath started an antislavery paper in Kansas called the *Crusader of Freedom*,[209] which was taking his life into his own hands; antislavery editors in Kansas were routinely lynched, beaten or bombed.

After John Brown's massacre of proslavery settlers at Pottawatomie, Kansas, Redpath received some tips and set out to find Brown for an interview. Finding him, they talked for about an hour—the first of many meetings between the men. Redpath fell under the spell of Brown and became an ardent follower.[210] Redpath shared Brown's belief that, if armed, slaves would fight for their freedom, and Brown soon enlisted Redpath in his plans to instigate a slave revolt.[211] Brown and his four sons attempted to start an insurrection in Kansas. Brown then attempted to foment a slave revolt in Virginia and hatched a doomed plan to seize the federal arsenal at Harper's Ferry, Virginia.

Redpath was apprised of the outline of the plot and was recruited by Brown to raise funds for him.[212] That same year, 1859, both Sojourner Truth and John Brown visited Redpath's Malden home.[213] Redpath did not reject violence in the war against slavery: "If we want to make good terms with the Slave Power, let us bring it on its knees first! And there is but one way of doing that: by attacking it where it is weakest—at home…one insurrection in Virginia in 1832 did more for the emancipation cause, than all the teachings of the Revolutionary Founders."[214]

Brown's raid on October 16, 1859, failed, and he was tried and promptly hanged. Redpath was enlisted to write a sympathetic account of Brown and promptly rushed into press *The Public Life of Capt. John Brown*.[215] He also collected and published a set of documents about Brown entitled *Echoes of Harper's Ferry*.[216] In December 1859, Congress launched an investigation into the raid. It turned up a letter confirming Redpath knew of Brown's plot.[217] Redpath was identified as a conspirator with Brown. Federal marshals served Redpath a summons to appear before Congress. Fleeing Malden to avoid arrest,[218] Redpath refused to appear before the Senate committee investigating the raid.[219] Redpath returned to his Malden home, determined to stand his ground: "I shall stay at home & fire at the first intruder on my premises.…That the body of a U.S. Marshal is not impervious to a bullet well directed, is a lesson that I think now needs to be demonstrated—and the times are ripe for it."[220] He never testified. Redpath made enemies seemingly everywhere and went out on the street armed.[221]

Haiti attracted Redpath as a possible place to resettle freed blacks and establish a black republic.[222] He was hired by the president of Haiti to publish a *Guide to Hayti* in 1861.[223] He also began a newspaper, the *Pine and the Palm*, dedicated to resettlement of black citizens in Haiti. Redpath called for the "immediate eradication of slavery" through a Constitutional amendment, the national equality and power of blacks and whites and the establishment of "tropical confederacies" in the Caribbean that, he believed, would encircle the slave power and attack the slave South.[224]

After the Civil War, Redpath was asked to become superintendent of schools in Charleston, South Carolina. It is here that some assign credit to Redpath as being the originator of what we know today as Memorial Day.[225] Redpath returned to Malden, where he began a lyceum bureau. The roster of Redpath's bureau included the most notable speakers of the day: Wendell Phillips, Susan B. Anthony, Frederick Douglass, Henry Ward Beecher, Julia Ward Howe, Charles Sumner, Mary Livermore, Edward Everett Hale, William Lloyd Garrison, Thomas Nast (the artist) and his biggest attraction, Mark Twain.[226] Years later, Redpath would serve as a secretary to Mark Twain in preparing his autobiography. Redpath also operated a small publishing company, which published Louisa May Alcott's first bestseller, *Hospital Sketches*.[227]

Redpath's home in Malden and his office on Bromfield Street in Boston both became something of intellectual salons where these notables would gather, smoke and talk.[228] Walt Whitman was a regular visitor to Redpath's home when he was in Boston.[229] Malden residents recalled Whitman and the Redpaths spending time after dinner at "Sunset Rock," conversing well past dark.[230] Redpath was also close with the Malden circle of reformers. He was intimate with Gilbert Haven, and in fact, Haven's Boston office was adjacent to Redpath's. The Redpaths frequently spent time with Harriet Hanson Robinson and her husband, William.[231] For a few years in the 1870s, Redpath was something of a gadfly in Malden politics.[232]

Redpath sold his lyceum bureau in 1875 and around that time moved away from Malden, spending time in Washington and New York. He was a Fenian and active in the movement for Irish independence.[233] He became editor of the *North American Review*.[234] Perhaps his last notable work was the several months he spent with Jefferson Davis, the former president of the Confederacy, gathering information for a biography of Davis. The two became intimate friends.[235] Redpath died on February 10, 1891, after having been struck by a vehicle while crossing Broadway in New York. As the *Boston Globe* recounted in 1888, "No one man ever held the friendship of so many people who radically differed from each other as has James Redpath."[236]

Gilbert Haven was an abolitionist and Methodist bishop.[237] He was born in 1821 in Malden, the son of "Squire" Gilbert and Hannah Haven. Squire Haven and his wife were abolitionists and subscribed to the antislavery cause in the early days. Haven also subscribed to these beliefs at an early age—when he saw his Malden schoolmaster beat a black girl, he confronted his teacher, saying, "If that girl had not been from the poor house and black, you wouldn't have dared to whip her as you did."[238] He used to say his mother and the Bible made him an abolitionist.[239] As a teenager, he clerked in a dry goods store with Eben D. Jordan, who later began Boston's great department store Jordan Marsh.

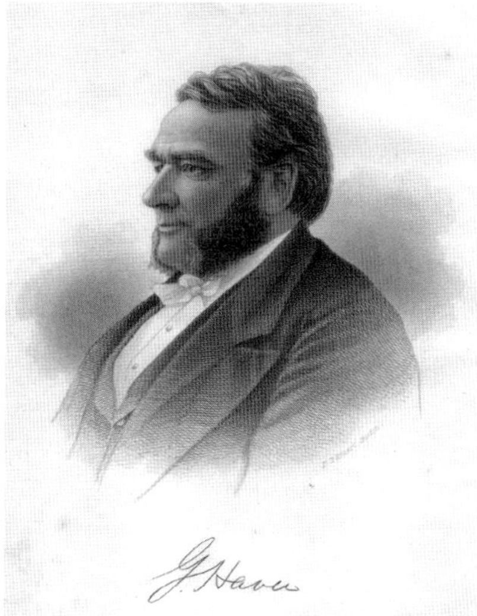

Gilbert Haven, the younger, was born in Malden. He was an abolitionist and a Methodist bishop. His grave is at the Salem Street Cemetery. *Author's collection.*

Haven left Malden and went to school in Wilbraham and a seminary in Amenia, New York, where he first developed his reformist thinking. Haven believed in interracial marriage when even abolitionists rejected such a belief. He said in one sermon, "When you ask us if we believe in the intermarriage of the races, we answer, 'true marriage is a divine institution.'"[240] He supported arming black soldiers to fight in the Civil War[241] and arming slaves.[242] He thought slavery could be extinguished by purchase and that the federal government owed reparations to slaves for their servitude.[243] Very few, even abolitionists, could sympathize with Haven's views on the absolute equality of blacks and whites. "He was out of sight ahead," wrote one biographer.[244]

Haven's first foray into political topics was a sermon criticizing the Fugitive Slave Law in 1850.[245] His sermon told listeners to "disobey" the act. As to the escaped slave, "[w]e must conceal him from his pursuers. We must aid him to escape."[246] Thus began a prolific outpouring of sermons, letters and speeches on abolition, race relations and other reform topics. By 1857, Haven was in Roxbury and became acquainted with the inner circle of Boston abolitionism: Wendell Philips, Lucy Stone and William Lloyd Garrison.[247] Like Redpath, Haven was also a friend to Sojourner Truth, whom he first met in Northampton and later entertained at his

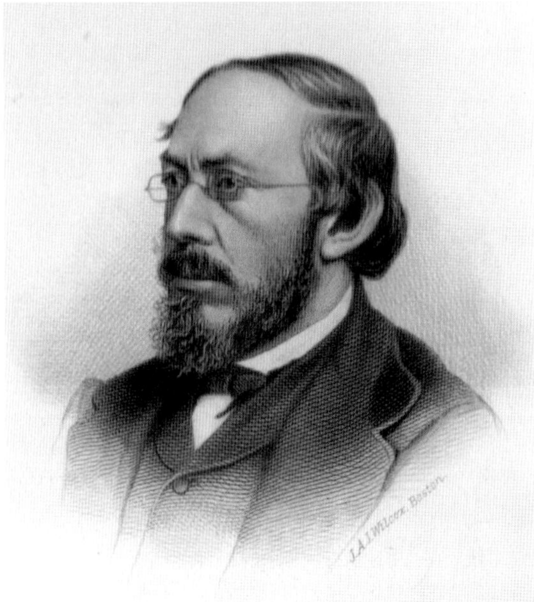

William S. Robinson was the husband of Harriet Hanson Robinson and was active in political and reform circles. *Malden Historical Society.*

home in Malden.[248] Haven believed the Civil War had a divine purpose: the beginning of an international brotherhood of man. In Haven's view, which broke from that of many antislavery people, slavery as well as racism itself needed to be eradicated.[249]

Haven returned in 1863 to reside in Malden, where he became a frequent speaker at abolitionist meetings. He spoke on the platform with Frederick Douglass in Boston's Tremont Temple in May 1863.[250] When Boston's black community sought to celebrate the anniversary of the Emancipation Proclamation in 1864 and 1865, it turned to Haven, who was invited to speak along with black abolitionists William Wells Brown and Joshua Smith and white abolitionists William Lloyd Garrison and George Thompson.[251] Haven contributed to the Boston Vigilance Committee, which aided escaped slaves.

Haven was the editor of the Methodist newspaper *Zion's Herald* from 1867 to 1872, during which he enlisted articles from, among others, Redpath and Malden's William S. Robinson, popularly known as "Warrington."[252] William S. Robinson was the husband of Harriet Hanson Robinson. Robinson himself was on good terms with many of the same reformers and politicians whom Redpath and Haven knew. Robinson became a power in Massachusetts politics and for many years was clerk of the House of Representatives.[253] Haven and Robinson became close friends based on their interest in similar reform movements. Whenever Haven returned to Malden, he would seek the company of Robinson to discuss the issues of the day.[254] Haven wrote numerous pamphlets and several books, including *National Sermons: Sermons, Speeches, and Letters on Slavery and Its War*, a collection of his abolitionist and reformist preaching and writings.[255]

In later years, he was sent to the South, where he worked with black students. He was an early benefactor of a black college, what is today Clark Atlanta University, where he raised funds for endowments and construction.[256] His death on January 3, 1880, was reported nationally. On the day of his funeral in the Centre Methodist Church, the bells of the various Malden churches tolled and business was generally suspended in the town.[257] Haven is buried at the Salem Street Cemetery.

Chapter 7

SATAN'S KINGDOM TUMBLING DOWN

MALDEN DURING THE CIVIL WAR

At a crowded meeting on April 20, 1861, it was "Resolved, That we believe it to be the duty of every lover of his country and his race to assist in crushing out the rebellion and treason now existing in the Southern states. Resolved, that the town of Malden, true to its ancient history, will furnish men and means to the extent of her ability for this object; and, we recommend the immediate formation of a company of volunteer militia to aid in preserving the government of the United States." Soon thereafter, volunteers began enlisting, and subscriptions were begun for equipment and supplies. A few days after the town meeting, another vote authorized spending $10,000 for the "comfort and support" of the families of those Malden residents called to serve in the military service.

Malden's volunteers formed into a company on May 6, 1861, and drilled in the town hall under the command of Captain Joseph R. Simonds and Lieutenant Ivory N. Richardson. On July 10, they were styled Company K, 17th Regiment, of the Massachusetts Volunteer militia and sent to camp at Lynnfield. The majority of Company K was Malden men, many of whom previously served in the Malden Light Infantry, the town's military company, but not all Malden men served in Company K.[258]

The first Malden man killed in the Civil War was Sergeant Gordon Forrest at Blackburn's Ford on July 18, 1861, a skirmish that preceded Bull Run.[259] Company K left Lynnfield for Baltimore on August 28, 1861, and arrived on September 1. Conditions in Baltimore kept the company there, where it performed guard duty.[260] On March 27, 1862, the company

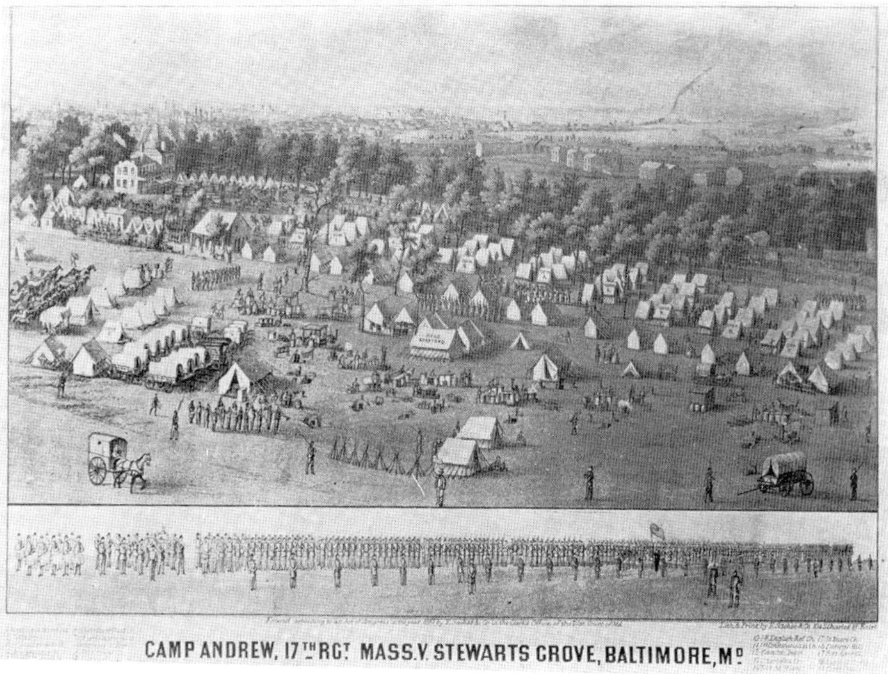

Company K was part of the 17th Regiment, Massachusetts Volunteer Militia. It encamped in Camp Andrew at Baltimore, seen here. *Author's collection.*

boarded a steamer for New Bern, North Carolina, where it performed picket duty. Company K saw most of its service in North Carolina during the war, where the entire 17th Regiment became part of the 1st Brigade of the 18th Army Corps.[261] Most of its action was between December 14 and 17, 1862, when it engaged in several battles on the march to Goldsboro. From October 1862 to February 1864, the company performed provost duty in New Bern. In February 1864, a detachment of eight officers and sixty-two men was ordered to aid Colonel Classen at Batchelder's Creek. In the meantime, Classen and his troops had retreated due to the overwhelming Confederate force, leaving the 17th Regiment to be captured. Of the sixty-two men captured, seven died in Confederate prisons, six of them from starvation at Andersonville.[262] Leverett D. Holden, for many years Malden's city clerk, was a private in Company H of the 1st Massachusetts Infantry. In a 1914 speech to the Malden Club, Holden recalled signing up on September 10, 1861, in Boston for a term of three years, "unless sooner shot."[263]

William H. Homans of Malden, who was white, was a first lieutenant in the famed black regiment the 54th Massachusetts, commanded by Robert Gould Shaw.[264] Wounded in the shoulder in the doomed assault on Fort Wagner, spitting up blood and thinking he was fatally injured, Homans staggered and was assisted to the rear.[265] Described as an "impetuous and brave" officer,[266] Homans was later promoted to captain of the 54th's Company C.[267] He was mustered out at the expiration of his term of service.[268]

There are two men buried in Malden cemeteries whose service in the Civil War is worthy of note, although they were not of Malden at the time. Colonel Moses B. Lakeman, buried at the Salem Street Cemetery, led the 3rd Maine Volunteer Infantry at Gettysburg, where it saw intense action in the Peach Orchard on July 2, 1863. George H. Harrison was awarded the Congressional Medal of Honor for valor while serving on the USS *Kearsarge* in its battle with the Confederate ship *Alabama* off the coast of Cherbourg, France. He is buried at Forest Dale Cemetery.[269]

Altogether, more than eight hundred Malden men served their country in the army and navy during the Civil War. Malden spent more than $60,000 in war charges, and townspeople raised an additional $25,000 through public meetings and charitable organizations.[270]

A Ladies' Soldiers Aid Society, organized in October 1861, was very active in Malden. For example, in 1862, more than four hundred people donated shirts, sheets, bedding and other articles for hospital use, "delicacies for the sick," fruit, sugar, jellies, tea, wines and spices.[271] On July 9, 1863, the united schoolchildren of Malden gave a gala concert at the town house to raise money for those in need. To be sure, during the war, women took a role in the workplace, filling the places of men in stores and farms and at the Boston Rubber Shoe Company plant, making footwear for the Union army under a government contract.

When the news reached Malden of General Lee's surrender to General Grant, the entire town welcomed the news. The day was recorded by Georgie Brown Mirick[272] of the Malden High School in a daily journal:

> *Monday, April 10. The dawn was ushered in by the ringing of bells and the booming of cannon on all sides, for news had arrived in the night of the surrender of the rebel Gen Lee and his army to brave Gen Grant on the 9th inst….Never, I think since the Revolution, has joy filled the hearts of so many as on this glorious day. The committee sent word by two damsels who had been dispatched to solicit this for a holiday that they had previously determined so to do and were soon to send word to that effect. We closed*

> *the exercises of the day by singing "Old Hundred." The school was then assembled at the door to give three cheers for Gen Grant. This was followed by 3 each for The Army of the Potomac, What they had accomplished, What they were going to do. 3 for father Abraham and last 3 each for Mr. D*[aniels] *and Miss Patch. We then dispersed some to the Cascade while others remained in the square. All were jubilant and manifested their joy by external demonstrations. The Star Spangled Banner not only floated from the several flag staffs, but from staffs fastened on to some part of every scholars apparel. The day is one long to be remembered in the annals of the town.*[273] *Satan's Kingdom tumbling down, Glory Hallelujah.*[274]

The jubilation would not last long. Another Malden High School student, L.L. Collins,[275] recorded on April 17: "A spirit of sadness brooded over the whole school. The terrible intelligence of Saturday was uppermost in the thoughts of all." President Abraham Lincoln had been assassinated.[276] The next day, Collins recorded, "The sun rose bright and clear this morning, but upon a nation bound with grief. Though many flags were playing with the breeze, they indicated sorrow, for they were at half-mast."[277]

Chapter 8

SHALL WE SUFFOCATE ED GREEN?

The Converse Murder

The relative peace of Malden during the Civil War was shattered on Tuesday, December 15, 1863, by the murder of Frank Converse, the son of Elisha and Mary Diana Converse.[278] Young Converse was seventeen years old and working as a teller in the First National Bank of Malden on Pleasant Street. The bank's cashier, Charles Merrill, had left Converse alone while he went into Boston to make a deposit. He left Converse with $5,000 cash in the bank's drawers, $3,000 of which was in $100 denominations. At about 11:00 a.m., Henry Stone went into the bank and transacted business; a Mr. Gray and the postmaster, Edward Green, were leaving the bank as he went in.[279] Converse was again left alone. Just after 11:30 a.m., George Bailey entered the bank to cash a check. He found Converse alone, reading a newspaper. Bailey cashed his check and left the bank. A few minutes before noon, fourteen-year-old Charles Merrill Jr., son of the cashier, entered the bank and found Converse on the floor, behind the counter, gasping for breath and bleeding from the head. He ran to get assistance. Dr. Burpee arrived but could not provide assistance, and Converse died shortly thereafter. Merrill recorded the scene in a letter to his friend Fred Hadley in San Francisco:

> *I suppose I must tell you that Frank has been murdered by some cruel person he was in the bank attending to his duty on Tuesday dec. 15. At about 25 minutes past 11 o'clock Mr. Bailey went in and exchanged some bills with Frank and he was alone. At about 20 minutes of 12 I went into the*

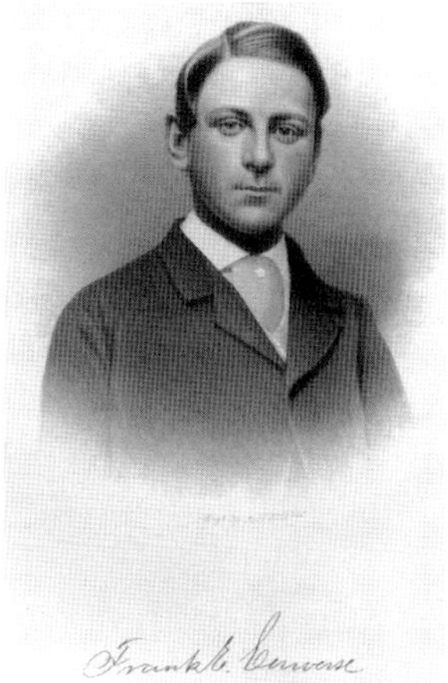

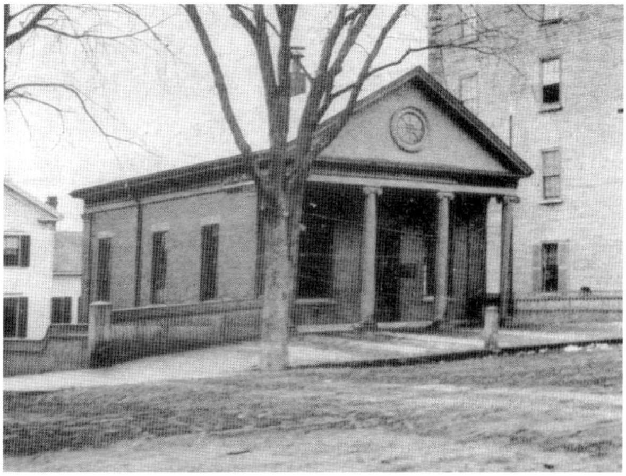

Left: Frank Eugene Converse was the son of Elisha Slade and Mary Diana Converse. He was murdered in December 1863 while working as a teller in the First National Bank of Malden. *Author's collection.*

Right: The First National Bank of Malden, built in 1851 on the corner of Pleasant and Middlesex Streets, was the scene of the Converse murder in 1863. *Malden Historical Society.*

> *bank to sit with Frank and when I got behind the counter I found Frank lying on the floor with blood coming out of his head he was groaning and struggling to breathe I immediately ran into Mr. Dowling shop and cryed for assistance then I ran after some doctors and doctor Burpee came first and said he was past doctors cure.*[280]

The balance of the $5,000 had been stolen from the bank.[281] No one had seen who committed the crime.

Converse's mother, Mary, was summoned from her home on Main Street, and Elisha Converse arrived from Boston. The parents were, as one may imagine, inconsolable. The town was stunned by the news, which spread rapidly. Frank Converse's former classmates at the high school were shocked. The day's high school journal entry, written by student Sarah F. Moody, reported, "At recess the scholars were thrown into a commotion by the news of a fearful tragedy which had just occurred. One who had been the schoolmate of many of us came to an untimely death by the hand of violence. Oh! What were a few thousand dollars compared with that young life."[282]

Immediately, rewards were posted for the recovery of the money. The town selectmen authorized a $500 reward for information leading to the apprehension of the killer.[283] The bank offered a $5,000 reward. The case caught the attention of the Boston and national press.

Initially, George Bailey, the son of Timothy Bailey, was accused and arrested for murder, having been, unfortunately, the last person seen in the bank. After a police court inquest that lasted two days, Bailey was acquitted and released from Charlestown jail. A large parade of townspeople rode out to welcome him back. More than one hundred members at a meeting of the people offered to pay Bailey's attorneys' fees for the unjust criminal case.[284]

Two police detectives from Boston were detailed to Malden to investigate the crime. Friends of the Converse family formed a "Secret Circle" to try to track down the killer. So far as we know, the Secret Circle consisted of Ezra D. Lamson, George D.B. Blanchard, Caleb Waite, Hubbard Russell (a selectman), John H. Abbott, Charles Sanderson and Charles Sprague. Suspicion began to center on the postmaster, Edward Green. Initially, Green, unlike the majority of his Malden neighbors, showed no feeling about the murder, never discussed it and never attended any meetings of the townspeople where the murder was the topic. This was noticed by the two detectives and several of his Malden neighbors. Then it was discovered that Green was heavily in debt. Green was a town agent for the sale of schoolbooks and, ironically, had been recommended as postmaster by Elisha Converse. He was in arrears on his account with the town. The Secret Circle soon began following Green. Members noticed that Green was suddenly able to pay a long-standing debt of $700—all in Malden Bank bills. He paid other, smaller debts, too—also in Malden Bank bills. Elisha Converse was informed of the suspicions. It was soon determined to arrest Green.

The Secret Circle met with the two detectives at Ezra Lamson's home, and a plan was hatched. Green was at B.F. Jackson's livery stable in Malden Center; it was agreed to arrest him as he left the stable. John Abbott met Green and invited him over to Ezra Lamson's. To Green's surprise, as he entered the Lamson home, there was the Secret Circle and the two detectives. Green was informed that he was under arrest for the Converse murder. Green was searched, and on him was found seventy-seven dollars in Malden Bank bills. He confessed to the murder. Green said that he was in the bank earlier and then returned later when Converse was alone. He pulled out his Smith & Wesson revolver and shot Converse twice, took the money in the bank and returned to the post office. Green disclosed the whereabouts of the hidden money to the Secret Circle. Some was secreted in a boot in the post office and the remainder under a floorboard in the attic of the "Volunteer" engine house. The Smith & Wesson was found in Green's boardinghouse.

It turned out that Green had been living beyond his means and had been using postal and schoolbook money to cover his mounting expenses.[285] Local legend also says that the local barber, Peter Shiloh, a black man, whose shop was also on Pleasant Street, saw everyone who entered the bank that day, including Edward Green. Shiloh did not see Green leave. Supposedly, Shiloh passed this information along to Elisha Converse, and as thanks, Converse paid to erect a dwelling house for Shiloh on Walnut Street.[286] A book about the murderer Green was rushed into print to satisfy the public's demand,[287] as was a broadside containing elegiac poetry eulogizing the victim, Converse.[288]

Green was indicted by a Middlesex County grand jury and scheduled for trial before a justice of the Supreme Judicial Court, which heard capital cases in those days. He was brought before Justice E.R. Hoar. Green initially pled guilty to second-degree murder, a charge that did not carry the death penalty. Hoar refused to accept the plea.[289] He instructed Green that he must either plead guilty to murder in the first degree or not guilty. Green retired

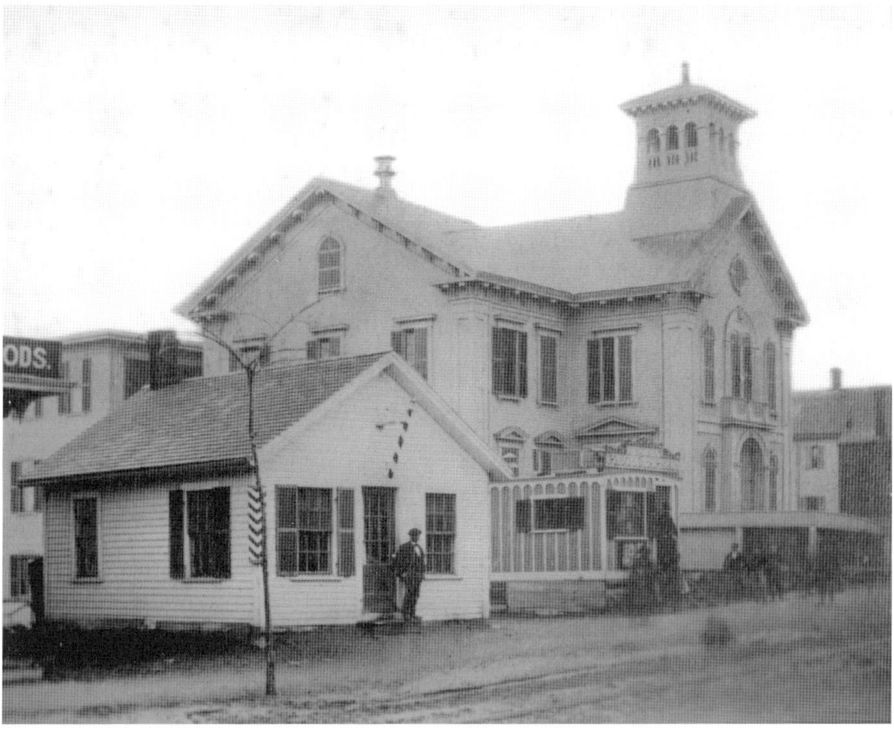

Peter Shiloh is seen in front of his barbershop on Pleasant Street. To the right E.C. Swain's photography studio and the Centre Grammar School. *Malden Historical Society*.

with his counsel and then pleaded guilty to murder in the first degree.[290] The plea was accepted by the court, and Green was sentenced to death. There was no trial.[291]

While it is generally accepted today that Converse was the first person killed in a bank robbery murder in America, the murder and trial are important for other reasons: the Green case precipitated a heated debate over the rightness of capital punishment in Massachusetts. James Redpath penned and published a diatribe against executing Green. Dedicated to Governor John Andrew, it was titled *Shall We Suffocate Ed. Green?*[292] Governor Andrew was a friend of Redpath's since the late 1850s. Andrew was also personally acquainted with Gilbert Haven, with whom he had discussed temperance and antislavery.[293] Andrew had been one of the founders of the Society for the Abolition of Capital Punishment and had asked the General Court in 1861 to abolish the death penalty.[294] To Andrew, that a criminal could sentence himself to the gallows, to "commit suicide by operation of law," was repugnant.[295] Redpath, Wendell Phillips, the Boston abolitionist and reformer Samuel Gridley Howe and others appeared before the Governor's Council to seek clemency for Green. Among them was another Malden minister, Reverend Thomas Greenwood of the Universalist church.[296] It was reported that the Converse family also did not desire Green's execution.[297]

The Governor's Council certified two major legal questions to the Supreme Judicial Court: (1) whether, on a guilty plea, it was appropriate for the trial judge to sentence the accused to death or whether the law required a jury trial nonetheless before death could be pronounced and (2) whether the guilty plea was sufficient to establish first-degree murder or whether the law required a jury to find the degree of guilt.[298] The Supreme Judicial Court held that Green's plea was sufficient to impose a death sentence on him and that a trial was not required.[299] Nonetheless, Governor John Andrew, an opponent of the death penalty, refused to sign Green's death warrant. Andrew asked the council to commute Green's sentence to life imprisonment; it refused.[300] He then undertook an investigation of the manner of the trial and the mental stability of Green, along with the legal issues involved.[301] Andrew's inaction, his failure to do what some saw as his duty as chief executive, angered many. "It is rumored here that the Governor shrinks from a duty that his oath should oblige him to perform," wrote one letter writer to the *Boston Journal*.[302] Handbills appeared on the streets of Boston demanding that the governor explain his refusal to hang "the Malden murderer."[303] Andrew completed his investigation near the end of his term. He again asked the council to commute the sentence, and again it refused.[304] Because of the controversy,

Andrew published his opinion on his refusal to execute Green.[305] In a letter, Andrew stated, "As to Green—I am doing my duty…[a]nd I am willing…to rest my whole reputation as a civil magistrate upon my conduct in that case alone."[306] It took the election of a new governor, Alexander H. Bullock, to sign Green's death warrant.[307]

Although Green's execution was set, with the encouragement of the now former governor Andrew, Green appealed and had his case brought before the Supreme Judicial Court on a writ of error.[308] The court reaffirmed its earlier decision.[309] A final, informal appeal was heard by Bullock and the Governor's Council in April 1866. Wendell Phillips appeared again to argue on Green's behalf, joined by others, including Malden's Gilbert Haven and Reverend Greenwood. Haven had known Green since he was a boy and claimed that Green had limited intellectual capacity.[310] Bullock was unmoved; Green was scheduled to hang three days later at the Charlestown prison.

Did Green suffer? He was placed in a noose, the trap was sprung and Green's body dropped, but the rope was too long and Green's toes touched the ground. Rather than having his neck snap, the husband and father was slowly strangled to death over a period of ten to twelve minutes.[311] Perhaps Redpath and Andrew were right.

Chapter 9

THE POSTBELLUM GROWTH OF THE TOWN

After the close of the Civil War, Malden's growth became exponential. The town report for 1864 found the three existing schools—the Centre, Walnut Street and West—insufficient for the growing population and noted that an additional building was needed west of the Boston & Maine railroad tracks. The fire department purchased its first steam engine to protect the 6,876 inhabitants of the town. In 1866, an armory was erected for the 3rd Battery of the Massachusetts Volunteer Militia on town land situated on Mill Street, later to be named Mountain Avenue. Sanitary conditions led to the creation of a board of health that year.

As the population expanded, the water supply became a source for concern for the town and a fertile source for political intrigue. In 1866, enterprising businessmen formed the Spot Pond Aqueduct Company with the intention of controlling the waters of Spot Pond and supplying them to the town. Elisha Converse was among them. The town opposed the plan, stating that it would adversely affect the dyeworks and the five hundred people dependent on that business for their employment, and therefore the plan was detrimental to the interests of the town as well. Malden filed a petition with the state legislature opposing the issuance of the license. Before the hearing, it was agreed that the towns of Malden and Melrose would each choose five members of the company, thus averting a controversy. By 1870, the Spot Pond waterworks was created, and an adequate supply of fresh water was introduced to the town.

The expense of water was also the source of controversy in South Malden. That the subject of separation of the southern part of the town was taboo is indicated by the rare mention of it in the town reports. Despite the simmering animosities, one of the few times it is mentioned is in the 1868 town report, which characterizes the issues as an "honest division of opinion." It was the only issue the selectmen had not acted on unanimously since 1864. As early as 1848, there was a proposal by members of the South District to be set off as a separate town, to be called Winthrop. More petitions were filed in 1849. Opposition was strong, however, since the southern part of the town contained the highest valuation of property. When North Malden also sought to be set off as a separate town of Melrose in 1850, a deal was struck whereby Malden did not oppose the separation of Melrose in return for its cooperation in opposing the separate incorporation of the southern part of the town.[312] Again in 1856 and 1857, petitions were filed to set off the southern part of Malden as a separate town to be called Winthrop but met with no success.[313] The issue slumbered until 1867, when renewed petitions were filed annually without success until 1870.

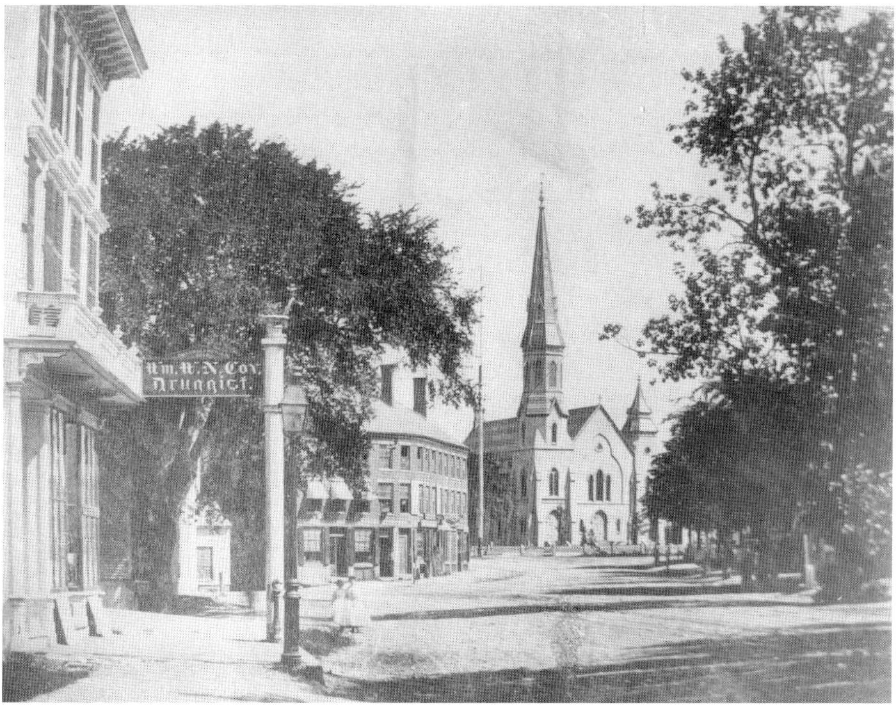

Malden Center in 1867. Here we see the brick Waite Block at the corner of Pleasant and Main Streets and the First Baptist Church in Converse Square. *Author's collection.*

By 1870, Hayes Atwood and others had filed another petition to set off the southern part of the town, this time to be called Everett, since the names Winthrop and Belmont—another choice—had by that time been taken. Malden appointed a committee to oppose the division, but to no avail. Also at the same time, Elisha Converse and others had filed a petition to annex the entire town of Malden to Boston. That petition was ultimately withdrawn.[314]

On March 9, 1870, a special act of the legislature set off the south precinct as the town of Everett with 2,200 inhabitants. This grant comprised the land obtained from Charlestown in 1726 called Mystic Side and the southeastern portion of the original town created in 1649. The movement for separation of the southern portion of the town had created ill feelings for more than twenty-five years. Six earlier attempts by the southern part to separate had failed. The separation in 1870 was vigorously opposed in Malden in a stormy town meeting. No wonder the town report bitterly stated of the separation "that it is an injury to us and them we believe they will soon acknowledge." The report predicted, "We do believe that the people of the new town of 'Everett' will be made aware of the fact before many years, that they made a great mistake in leaving the old 'Mother Town,' who however they claim otherwise, always treated them friendly, never having any ill-feelings towards them, as they assert, but rejoicing in their prosperity and our own."

The residents of South Malden, obviously, did not agree. After Everett was set off, Malden was left with 7,370 inhabitants.

Smaller villages began to be built up in Malden at Faulkner, Maplewood and Linden, along the stops of the Saugus Branch Railroad and at Belmont Hill and Oak Grove. At the same time, a contemporary commentator noted the "vigorous community of mechanics and laborers" that had developed in Edgeworth near the factories. Large estates began to appear in Malden as Boston businessmen moved to Malden, an easy commute to Boston. For example, on Pleasant Street, the estates of Stevens, Wiggin, Abbott, Burpee and Fall all had large homes and ornamental lawns. Others would recall some areas as slums: the "Rat Hole," a tenement located at the foot of old Abbott Street; Yankee Village, where the gas company was located; and the Marsh, in the area of Middlesex, Jackson and Charles Streets.[315] In 1877, two hundred acres of land in Medford, having about one hundred people, were added to Malden. The Linden Land Company began marketing house lots in Linden, south of Salem Street and in part of Revere. To accommodate new families, the Linden Land Company petitioned the town to erect a school, stating that it would donate ten thousand square feet of land for the purpose. In 1872 alone, twenty-six families with fifty-six children moved into new Linden homes. The company projected building another thirty houses the following year.[316] Within the next two years, Malden would erect the two-room Linden School, a two-room school at Oak Grove and a four-room Judson School in the Belmont Hill area.

Growth in population also resulted in an increase in crime and disorder. Beginning in the 1850s, the town employed night watchmen. One of the earliest records is contained in an 1858 town report that shows three men paid for "services as watchman," "watching" and "night police."[317] The town seems to have maintained four to five watchmen during the 1860s.[318] By 1874, the *Malden Mirror* was calling for the appointment of a police chief and a permanent location for a police department.[319] The 1875 town report noted that with the large increase in population and the "free sale of intoxicating liquors," the need for a police department was also increasing. Yet the selectmen concluded that "the expense which it would involve has deterred us from carrying the measure into effect."[320] Apparently, the town created a police department the following year, as the *Mirror* reported that a police chief was appointed and a room provided in the town house.[321]

The job was dangerous. In December 1868, watchman David Faulkner was on patrol with his partner, George Chase, near the Malden Station when they came upon two suspicious men. Faulkner and his partner split up. Chase heard Faulkner address one of the men and then heard the report of a pistol. Faulkner was shot dead at the scene. His murderer was never caught.[322]

In November 1872, the town mourned firefighter Walter S. Trombly, who was killed fighting the Great Boston Fire. On November 9, 1872, while firefighters were attempting to rescue someone at Hixon's furniture store on Washington Street, a wall of the building collapsed, burying Trombly under the rubble. Three Malden fire companies participated: the Wannalancet, Daniel Webster and Hook and Ladder. Each company had men injured.[323]

The largest enterprise in Edgeworth—and indeed the entire town—was the Boston Rubber Shoe Company. Established in 1853, it enjoyed rapid growth in the 1870s. Malden suffered with the rest of the country during the depression that began in 1873 and lasted for several years. In November 1875, the Boston Rubber Shoe factory was destroyed by fire, causing grave concern among those who could least afford to lose their jobs in the poor economy. The corporation supported the employees through the rough winter of 1875–76 until new factories and machinery were constructed.

The growth of the town and the arrival of middle-class residents spurred agitation for a public library. The absence of a public library had led to

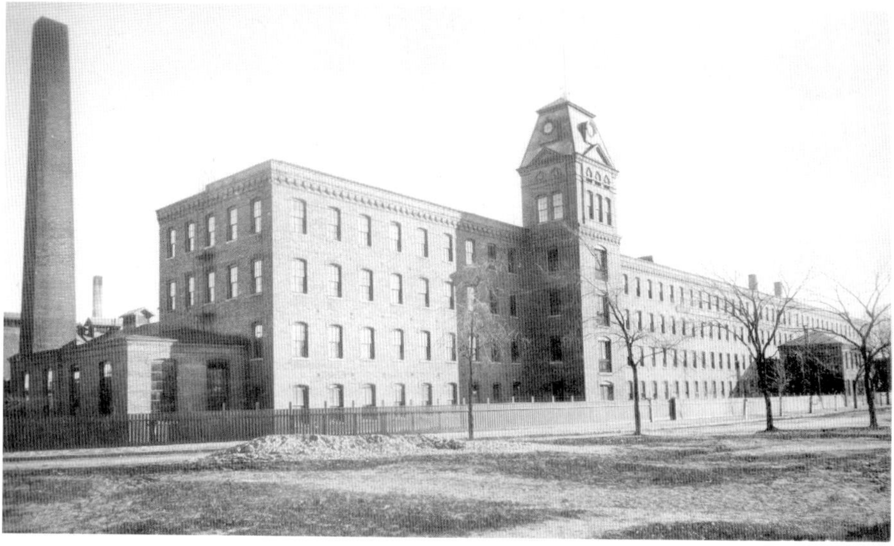

The Boston Rubber Shoe Company mill at Edgeworth, built in 1876 to replace the earlier brick factory that was destroyed by fire in November 1875. *Malden Historical Society.*

the creation of a library at Malden High School in 1864.[324] As early as 1871, a movement for a public library began but was quashed; many felt that it would strain town finances. In 1876, William Merrill proposed the idea of a library, and on April 1 of that same year, a bequest of $5,000 was received from John Gardner. Gardner was a native of Malden who, after the bequest to found a library, left the balance of his estate to the United States government. Merrill and the Malden Deliberative Assembly solicited funds and held a fair, and the Harvard Glee Club gave a concert to raise money.[325] In 1877, the town voted to start a library, and by 1879, a room was fitted up in the town house. The library opened on February 14, 1879, and remained in the town house until the opening of the Converse Memorial Building in 1885.

Searching for a suitable memorial to their slain son, Frank, Elisha and Mary Converse settled on a memorial library and art gallery. They selected the preeminent architect of the day, Henry Hobson Richardson. Constructed in Richardsonian Romanesque style, the memorial is nothing short of magnificent.[326] Richardson collaborated with Frederick Law Olmsted on the selection of the site for the library. Olmsted designed the courtyard garden. At one point, the Converses, who were members of the First Baptist Church, had contemplated hiring Richardson to design a new Baptist church edifice to complement the library.[327] Richardson drew up plans, but the church was

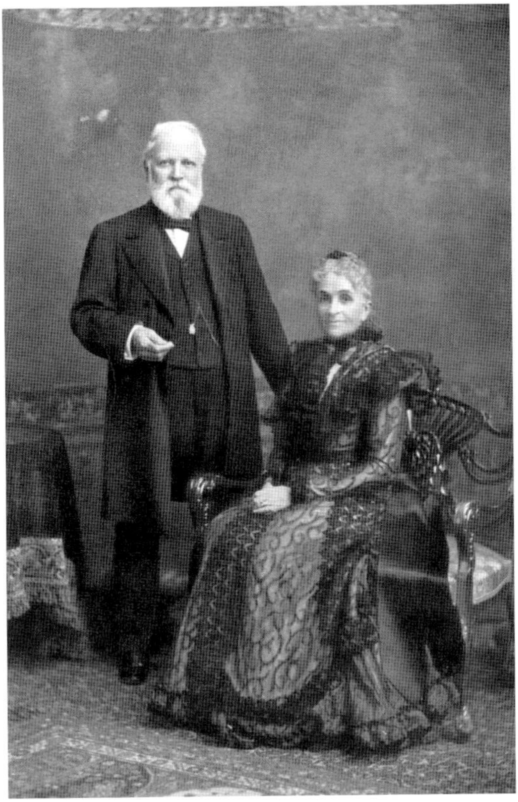

Left: Elisha Slade and Mary Diana Converse in a photograph taken for Malden's 250th anniversary in 1899. They donated the Converse Memorial Building in memory of their son, Frank. *Author's collection.*

Below: The Converse Memorial Building of the Malden Public Library, designed by Henry Hobson Richardson as a memorial to Frank Eugene Converse. It opened in 1885. *Malden Historical Society.*

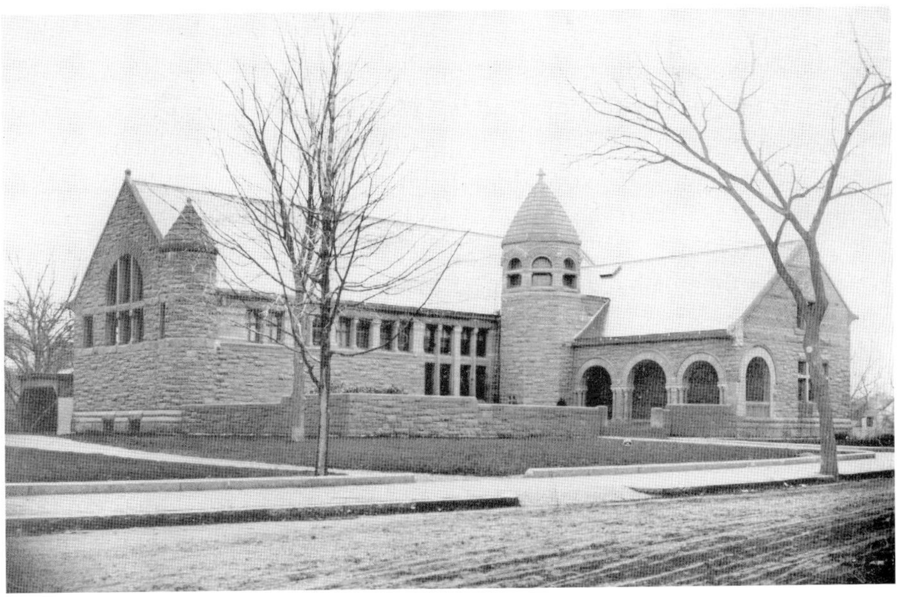

ultimately designed by H.S. McKay.[328] The oak furniture throughout the library building was specifically designed to complement the architecture and was manufactured by A.H. Davenport of Malden.[329] Today, it is believed to be the largest collection of Richardson-designed, Davenport-crafted furniture still residing in the building for which the furniture was designed.[330]

A portrait of Frank Converse by Albion Bicknell was commissioned for the building. The layout of the structure and the placement of the Converse painting, looking down the barrel-vaulted arch toward his parents' church, is not by accident—it was meant to convey a sense of mourning and death serving life. As Kenneth Breish described it, "In the spirit of late nineteenth-century public mourning ritual, the visitor to the Malden library is consciously led along a picturesque architectural path, from the domain of nature, through the realm of death and commemoration, to the altars of intellect and culture."[331]

This theme of death serving life was reflected in the remarks of Elisha Converse at the memorial's dedication in 1885: "In presenting this building, it is intended that it shall not only be a memorial to a young man summoned early from earth to heaven, but also in some sense a perpetuation of the work which he might have done as a citizen in this community had it pleased God to prolong his earthly life. It was the hope and belief of his parents that he would have taken an active part in the affairs of the town, and have joined heartily in the efforts of public-spirited men to promote the prosperity and welfare of Malden. Absent from our sight, we would have him present in his influence for good."[332]

The establishment of the library was not without controversy. Some citizens, led by Judge John Pettingill, objected to the library's charter, its private nature and its self-perpetuating board of trustees. A large public meeting filled the roller-skating rink on Main Street. After listening to Pettingill's objections, Converse delivered a passionate speech in favor of the library that was greeted with tremendous applause and cheers. The issue was settled, and the library went forward.[333]

The Massachusetts court system came to Malden in 1874 with the establishment of the First District Court of Eastern Middlesex, which had jurisdiction over cases arising in Malden, Medford, Melrose, Everett and Wakefield. It was located on the second floor of Sargeant's Block at the corner of Main and Ferry Streets.[334] After two other locations, a new court building was erected in 1899 at the corner of Pleasant Street and Linden Avenue, where the court occupied the second floor. The court moved to its present location on Summer Street at Mountain Avenue in 1922.

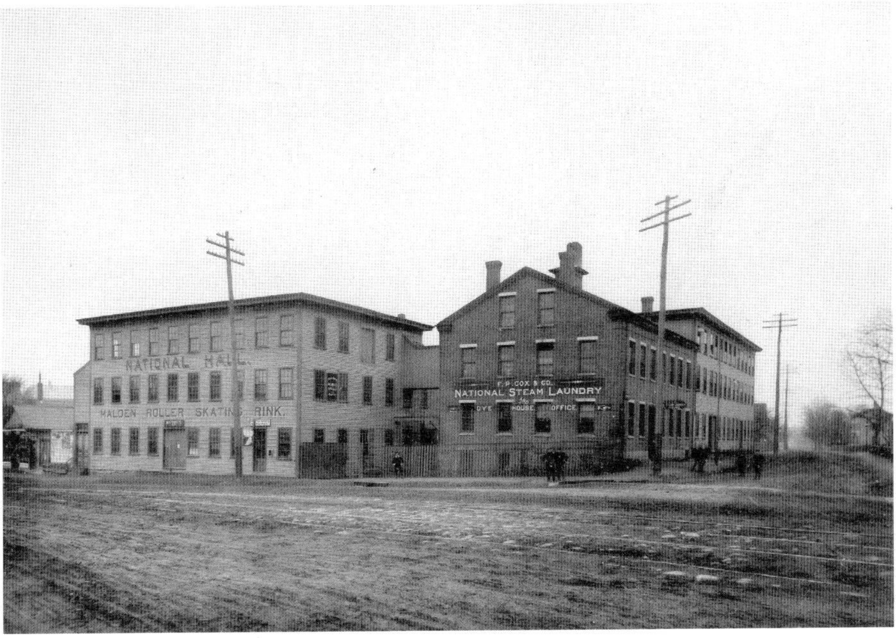

The roller skating rink, site of the great library meeting, is at left. The F.P. Cox cleaners and Eastern Avenue are at right. *Malden Historical Society.*

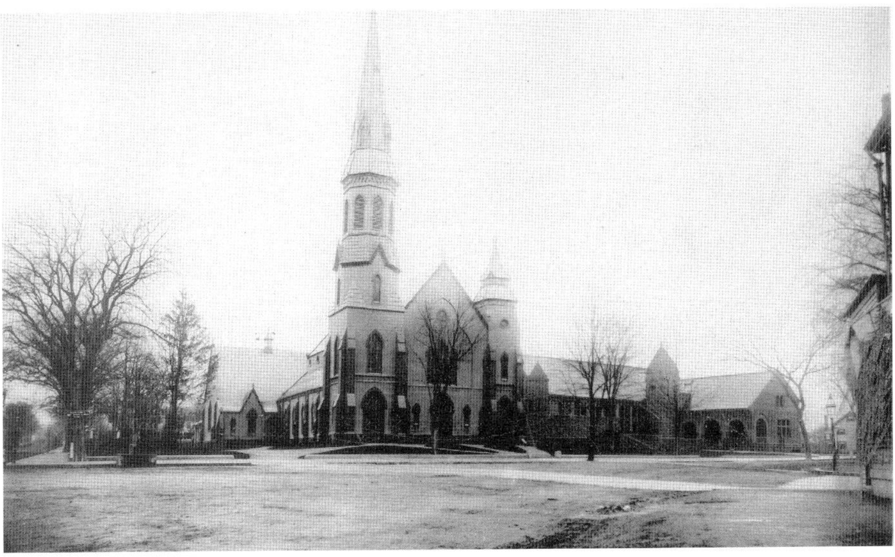

Converse Square in 1886. The First Baptist Church is located at the corner, and the Converse Memorial Building is to the right. *Malden Historical Society.*

Gradually, Malden was becoming enveloped by the expanding metropolis of Boston. The Middlesex Horse Railroad operated a horsecar line from Pleasant Street, down Main Street, through Charlestown to Boston's Scollay Square, running at fifteen-minute intervals. Tow boys were a common sight. The boys would hitch extra horses to the cars to enable them to climb the hills. Cars going southerly on Main Street had extra horses added at Madison Street so they could make it to Belmont Street.[335] Similar conditions prevailed at Linden for cars going up the hill on Beach Street.[336] In 1871, the fare to Everett was six and a half cents with a ticket or eight cents without; the price was ten cents to go all the way to Boston.[337] The horsecar stables were situated at the corner of Pleasant Street and the original Abbott Street and later became the Strand Theater. Open cars were used in the summer and closed cars in the winter. These horsecars gradually gave way to electric streetcars beginning in 1894 on a line from Belmont Street to Malden Square via Ferry Street.

Chapter 10

MALDEN

A City

With the rapid growth of the town evident, in 1880 prominent citizens began to consider the adoption of a city form of government once Malden's population reached the required threshold of twelve thousand. In March 1881, the legislature passed a special act granting a city charter to Malden that was accepted by the town meeting on June 9, 1881, thus ending the New England town meeting form of government that had run the town of Malden since its inception. The last board of selectmen consisted of George W. Walker, John P. Holden, Tristram Griffin, John M. Devir and John W. Allen.

A trend among the larger Massachusetts towns—Brockton having been the most recent—had spurred the pride of Malden's civic leaders to consider becoming a city. "No sensible man can read the [proposed city charter] document through and doubt that the administration of a city government is superior to that of a town with a population as large as ours," the *Malden Mirror* opined the Saturday before the vote.[338] Opponents of cityhood, the *Mirror* charged, were backward-looking. "If their ideas should be adopted grass would soon grow in the center of the streets of Malden, and the sound of wheels and steam would be heard no more," it editorialized. "These gentlemen are fortunately in a minority—a weak and sickly minority—and will never be able to accomplish more than to gush over relics of antiquity.... What has been is nothing compared with what will be."[339]

But there was more specific discontent with Malden's current town government that underlay the city charter push as well. Town meeting was run by a very few, and it paid little attention to detail. Spending habits were out of control, charged the *Malden Press*. "At our last Town Meeting, out of some 2,500 voters, only 148 voted on a money matter that had excited the attention of the town for weeks," the *Press* reported. "On this same evening, some seven or eight thousand dollars were appropriated for various purposes, the merits of which the voters as a body knew absolutely nothing."[340]

Malden's tax rate had risen from $10.50 per $1,000 of property value in 1879 to $10.80 in 1880 and was likely to be "not less than $13.50" in 1881, based on the town meeting's spending proclivities and "probably will be more than this," the *Press* said. "The time devoted to the consideration of [the budget] was less than an hour and a half; and little or no consideration was given to the needs or merits of the questions at issue."[341] Thus, argued the *Press*, Malden should become a city with professional men running its government. "The appropriations can and must be closely scrutinized by men chosen with especial reference to their qualifications in this respect, and whose sense of responsibility will prompt them to see that every sum voted out of the treasury is wisely expended."[342]

Yet even with such powerful historical and fiscal arguments, and the power of the town's two newspapers firmly behind cityhood, the vote on Tuesday, June 9, 1881, was far from overwhelming. Of 1,301 voters who showed up for town meeting, 801 chose cityhood and 500 voted to remain a town. The vote was "greeted with tumultuous applause," reported the *Mirror*.[343] The *Press*, now renamed the *Malden City Press* in honor of the victory, was magnanimous. "That those who, for what they deemed good and sufficient reasons, opposed the acceptance of the charter, will loyally acquiesce in the result, there can be no doubt....All parties at least will agree in giving expression to a feeling of satisfaction that the subject has finally been set to rest."[344] Of course, there was the resort to practical outlooks. "Time will prove that, with good men in office, the people's money can be made to go as far, and can be expended as wisely, under a city as under a town government, and that taxes will not be at a higher rate for the same improvements."[345]

The first city government was elected in December 1881 and inaugurated on January 2, 1882, for a term of one year. Elisha Converse was elected the first mayor by a wide margin.[346] The charter also created a bicameral legislature consisting of a board of aldermen and a common council. One alderman was elected at-large, and one alderman was elected for each of six wards. The common council was made up of eighteen members, three elected from each of the six wards. The first board of aldermen consisted of at-large alderman Benjamin Faulkner and Tristram Griffin, former selectman John

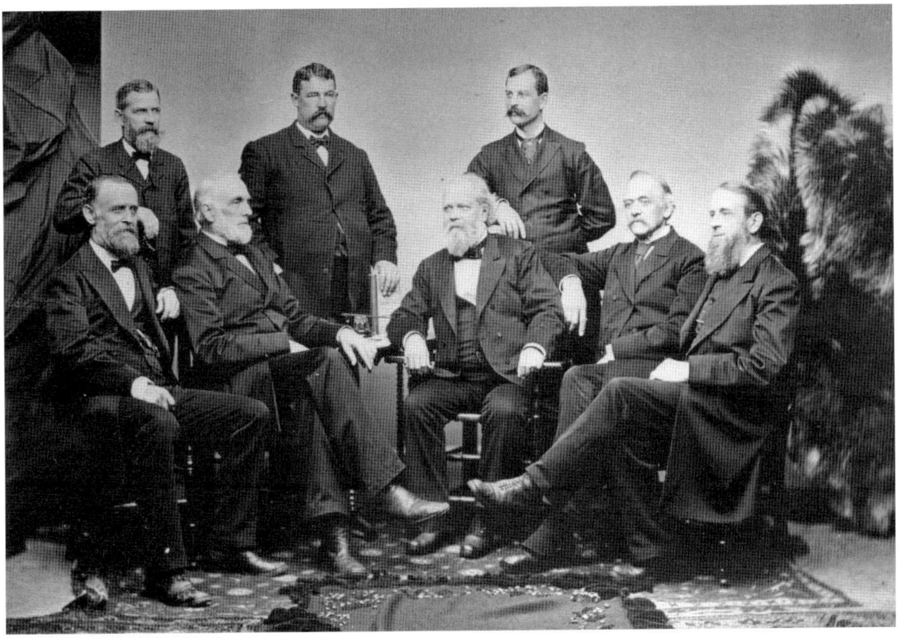

Malden's first board of aldermen in 1882. *From left to right:* Joseph M. Russell, Tristram Griffin, Lorin L. Fuller, John M. Devir, Mayor Elisha Converse, Frank M. Clark, George T. Coverly and Benjamin Faulkner. *Author's collection.*

M. Devir, Joseph M. Russell, George T. Coverly, Lorin L. Fuller and Frank M. Clark from wards one through six, respectively. By 1889, Malden was divided into seven wards, and the alderman-at-large position was abolished. The new city charter also created a nine-member school committee with the mayor as chairman ex-officio.[347] Although mayors were initially elected based on the candidate, not the party, for a brief period the Republican Party nominated candidates for the office of mayor who were opposed by the Independents.

The new city form of government paralleled a growth in Malden's population and the type of people moving into the city. If there ever was a time when Malden flirted with the rich and famous, it was the late nineteenth century and early twentieth century, when many fine residences were built by families of means. A turn-of-the-century guidebook noted that "many of Boston's most successful merchants reside here."[348] To ensure that readers knew Malden was home to the "better" classes, the guidebook added that the average annual majority voting against liquor licenses totalled 1,100.[349]

Malden's first citizen, Elisha Converse, lived in a large estate on Main Street at the Everett line. Furniture magnate Albert H. Davenport constructed an elaborate home on Salem Street opposite the high school. Benjamin F. Dutton, principal of the large Boston department store Houghton & Dutton, was ensconced in his mansion at Glen Rock. Situated at the head of Summer Street near the Middlesex Fells Reservation, Glen Rock was an estate in the true sense of the word. With expansive grounds, it consisted of a main house, enormous barn, gardens, arbors, grape house, tennis court and homes for relatives.[350]

Other notable estates, so picturesque that they warranted inclusion in a souvenir photographic book of Malden, included those of George Marshall at the corner of the Fellsway and Maple Street, Alexander McGregor Jr. at Glen Rock, Marcus Beebe at Pleasant Street and Highland Avenue, Daniel Wise on Webster Street and Frederick A. Robinson on Hancock Street.[351] In 1895, Eugene Nelson built the Ledges on Glenwood Street at Summer Street. Most of these remain today, with the exception of the Beebe estate. Only its granite wall at Wallace Park remains.

The wealthy in Malden also built magnificent summer houses to escape what was fast becoming a city and to keep in contact with fashionable circles. Albert H. Davenport escaped to his summer retreat at Squirrel Island, Maine, where he was also responsible, in large part, for the island's development as a summer resort.[352] Elisha Converse's son Harry Converse built a palatial Shingle-style estate in Marion on what is called Converse Point.[353] Charles Binner had a notable summer home at Pocasset in Bourne, Massachusetts.[354]

Despite the arrival of a wealthy class, at the city's 250th anniversary, a popular history reported that "Malden is not a city of the rich and, indeed, is not a rich city…but its industrial establishments offer fairly remunerative employment to hundreds."[355] Malden was described as a "home city," a pleasant place for people to live and "bring up their children in favorable surroundings."[356] Yet Malden did not escape the problems and misfortunes of an urban community. The Malden District Court docket handled cases of spousal abuse, drunkenness and juvenile delinquency. This was, as Anna Christy Fall wrote, a view of Malden not often seen.[357]

Chapter 11

ARTS AND LETTERS

Toward the end of the nineteenth century, as the more affluent members of the Boston business community built homes in Malden, the city developed a small colony of artists of unusual notoriety. Chief among them, perhaps, was Albion Harris Bicknell, a prominent landscape and portrait artist who moved his house and studio to Malden. Bicknell studied at the École des Beaux-Arts in Paris and opened a studio in Boston associated with William Morris Hunt, Thomas Robinson and Joseph Ames. His portraits were done for many state governments and the Treasury Department in Washington.[358] Bicknell published a portfolio of etchings in 1887. Involved in the elite Malden circles, he was the favorite artist of the Converse family and received several commissions from them. He painted many of the portraits that hang in the Converse Memorial Building, including the mammoth allegorical painting *Lincoln at Gettysburg*.

Horace Robbins Burdick was a well-known Boston artist in the late nineteenth century. He and his wife moved to Malden at the request of Charles Sprague, and his wife liked Malden so much they stayed.[359] No doubt Bicknell's presence in Malden added to Burdick's liking for the town. Bicknell's home housed a studio and, over it, a large billiard room where Bicknell, Burdick and other Boston artists gathered to play.[360] Burdick painted still lifes and portraits and was sought after to copy other paintings, as well as being a restorer of damaged artwork.[361] His daughter, Doris, became an accomplished silhouette artist and resided in her father's home on Park Street until her death in 1981.[362] Noted Boston Impressionist painter George

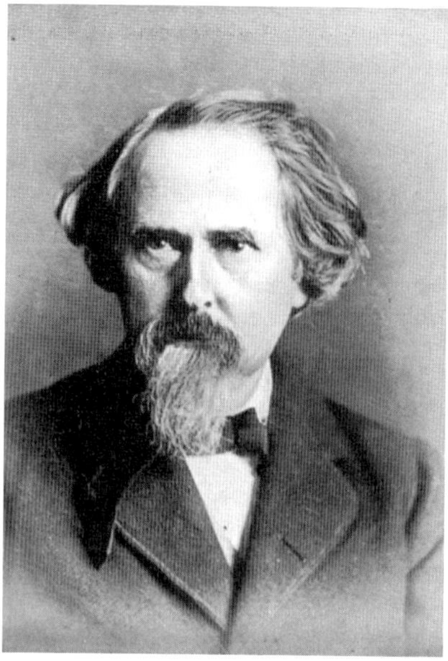

Malden artist Albion Harris Bicknell. His home was a gathering place for artists. *Malden Historical Society*.

Loftus Noyes resided with his brother in Malden between 1892 and the early 1900s.[363] George Loring Brown, famous for his Italian landscapes and views, also made his home in Malden.

Still another prolific artist was the Frenchman Joseph Morviller. Morviller came to Boston in 1852 and moved to Russell Street in Malden, where he lived between 1855 and 1870. Morviller was noted especially for his winter scenes, and Malden was the subject of several of his paintings. The itinerant painter Richard Henry Fuller of Chelsea was also fond of Malden scenes. He painted several of Edgeworth in the 1860s, two of which, *Edgeworth—Near Medford* (1867) and *View—Malden* (circa 1865), are in the collection of Boston's Museum of Fine Arts. These sublime views recall the bucolic farmland that once was Edgeworth. Theodore Marsden was well known for his drawings of horses, hunting and field sports. Marsden worked for a time as an illustrator for Boston lithographer John H. Bufford.

There was an art gallery in the home of C.O. Elliett at 64 Lyle Street in Oak Grove, where Burdick, Noyes and others exhibited.[364] Many of the Malden artists were members of the Boston Art Club and exhibited there. They also exhibited in the new art galleries of the Converse Memorial Building.

For those who could not afford art but appreciated it just the same, Eugene Perry had a solution. The headmaster of the Centre Grammar School began selling halftone reprints of images of famous people, paintings, buildings and scenes in 1897. The Perry Pictures were a phenomenal success and could be found in almost every home and school across America. "No one was too rich and no one was too poor" to own a Perry Picture.

Albert H. Davenport was born in Malden in 1845. Purchasing the Boston Furniture Company in 1880, he renamed it A.H. Davenport & Company. He became famous for producing his high-end, custom-made furniture for some of the wealthiest clients in America.[365] The company had a factory in East Cambridge and showrooms in Boston and New York. It worked

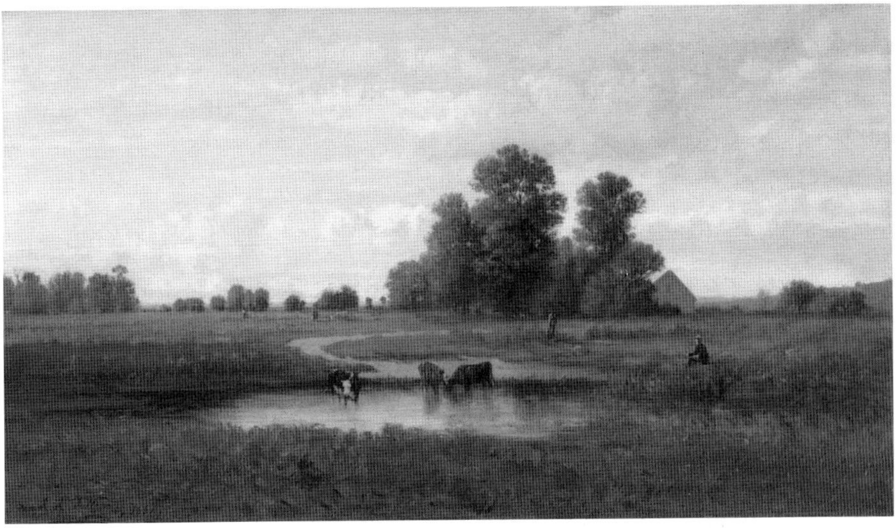

Richard Henry Fuller's painting *Edgeworth—Near Medford* (1867) gives a sense of the bucolic nature of Edgeworth before it was carved into house lots. *Museum of Fine Arts, Boston.*

with some of the leading architects of the day to execute their furniture designs. We have already noted Davenport-produced and H.H. Richardson-designed furniture for the Converse Memorial Building. It also produced Richardson-designed furniture for the Crane Library in Quincy and the Billings Library in Burlington, Vermont. Davenport also produced highly carved cabinetwork and furniture for Richardson's famous New York Court of Appeals. It produced the furniture and interiors for the 1896 addition to the Massachusetts State House.[366]

An early commission was for 225 pieces of furniture for the Iolani Palace in Hawaii. During Theodore Roosevelt's administration, the New York architects McKim, Mead & White designed renovations to the White House. A.H. Davenport was selected to execute the furniture designed by Stanford White for the State Dining Room and McKim-designed furniture for the Family Dining Room, Executive Office and Cabinet Room. Davenport built his magnificent mansion in 1892 on Salem Street near the Converse Memorial Building. Davenport died in 1905. The general term "davenport" for a piece of furniture originated with this company.

Alderman and selectman Tristram Griffin was a noted architect who resided in a Stick-style house at the corner of Bell Rock Street and Converse Avenue. He designed many homes and public buildings in Malden and Greater Boston.

Amateur theater flourished in Malden. The Malden Megatherians entertained audiences for nearly a decade, beginning in the 1890s. The Malden and Kernwood clubs performed amateur theatricals. In the early twentieth century, Malden theaters had their own stock companies. For example, the Temple Stock Company and the Auditorium Players performed at the Auditorium Theatre. The outdoor Boulevard Theatre was established on the Fellsway in Medford and Barrett's Opera House on Main Street, opposite the Baptist church. Many went to the theater and heard the popular song "Sweet Adeline," written and published by Malden native Harry Armstrong in 1903.

Chapter 12

ENVIRONMENTALISTS, SUFFRAGISTS AND SOCIALISTS

Until the 1890s, Malden was deficient in its provision of public park spaces. As late as 1882, the Malden Improvement Association determined that only two areas—what are today Sheridan Park and Amerige Field—were reserved for public parks, and those areas were reserved by private developers: the Edgeworth and Malden Highlands land companies, respectively.[367] Prior to that time, only the small triangle, now called the Harris Delta, was reserved for public recreation.[368] In the 1890s, Sylvester Baxter began to agitate for more park and playground spaces. "There is needed…a sufficient number of small local pleasure grounds, to meet the wants of the various neighborhoods in the way of breathing space," Baxter wrote in 1894.[369]

Baxter was a remarkable resident and defies characterization. Born in West Yarmouth on Cape Cod in 1850, Baxter attended the university in Leipzig before returning to America to become a columnist for the *Boston Herald*. He was a journalist, poet, author, art critic and environmentalist, among many other interests.[370] His writing was prolific and varied. He could write about art, such as Chelsea tile,[371] Japanese pottery[372] or Isabella Stewart Gardner's Fenway Court.[373] He was just as at home discussing municipal government in Germany[374] or city planning in Boston.[375] He was a close friend of Walt Whitman's.[376] Perhaps his most noteworthy works are a lavishly illustrated history of Spanish colonial architecture in Mexico[377] and his work on the archaeological expedition to the American Southwest with Frank Hamilton Cushing.[378] Baxter's monument, however, is the parks of Greater Boston.

Baxter had been instrumental in the establishment and protection of the Middlesex Fells. Medford's Elizur Wright began the agitation for preservation of the Fells and, with Baxter's assistance, carried the call to the state legislature.[379] Indeed, it was Baxter who coined the name Middlesex Fells for the rocky, wooded natural area north of Malden.[380] But perhaps Baxter's greatest achievement was his plan for a metropolitan park system in Boston. Together with landscape architect Charles Eliot, Baxter coauthored the pioneering *Metropolitan Park Report of 1893*, which offered a new vision of open spaces and parks for metropolitan Boston,[381] and became secretary of the Metropolitan Park Commission. He authored an early guide to the parks in Boston and its surrounding towns.[382] Baxter died in 1927 in San Juan, Puerto Rico.

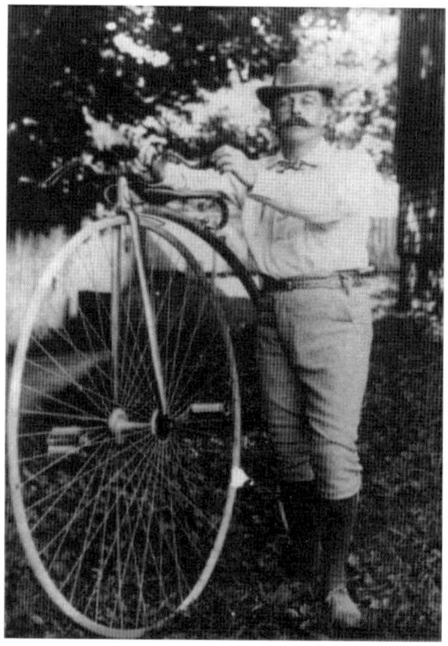

Sylvester Baxter was Malden's peripatetic author, poet, journalist, environmentalist, urban planner and reformer. *Malden Historical Society.*

The acquisition and development of Baxter's Malden breathing grounds took longer than the creation of the Middlesex Fells. Waite's Mount was purchased for water supply purposes in 1889, but there was so much land that it was transferred from the water department to the park department in 1893.[383] At about the same time, James F. Eaton gave land where wells were situated for purposes of a water supply and recreation. This became known as Webster Playstead (today's Roosevelt Field).[384] In 1892, ex-mayor John K.C. Sleeper donated three acres of land in the west end for a park provided that the reservoir of the Boston Rubber Shoe Company and other lands were made available. This land was developed into Fellsmere Park.[385] By 1894, the city had acquired other lands for park purposes, namely Devir Park (originally called Craddock Field), Coytemore Lea and Ferryway Green (originally called Hitching's Field). Pine Banks Park was privately owned by the Converse family, but its grounds were opened to the public.

Baxter, as a member of the Malden Park Commission, was instrumental in commissioning Frederick Law Olmsted and his firm to prepare the landscape design for several of Malden's new parks. Among those parks the Olmsted firm had a hand in designing were Fellsmere, Coytemore Lea,

Devir (Craddock's Field) Bell Rock, Ferryway (Hitching's Field) and the Harris Delta (Oldway Place).[386]

Also active in the park movement was William Beltran deLasCasas, who was appointed to the Metropolitan Park Commission in 1892 and became its chairman in 1895. His father, Francisco Beltran deLasCasas, was a Spanish revolutionary who was active in the movement for Cuban independence. In the 1880s, William began to acquire large real estate tracts in the West End and Oak Grove that he developed into fine residences. The streets now bear his family names as Francis, Beltran and LasCasas Streets.

The Middlesex Scientific Field Club was organized in Malden in 1878 and in 1881 changed its name to the Middlesex Institute. It was an organization of amateur naturalists and botanists. When the Converse Memorial Building was planned, space was originally included for the institute.[387] It published *Flora of Middlesex County* in 1888. Among its members were George Putnam Huntington, the first rector of St. Paul's Church and an amateur botanist, and Frank Shipley Collins, an employee of the Boston Rubber Shoe Company, who gained fame in his studies of North American algae.

In 1859, Harriet Hanson Robinson and her husband, William, moved from Concord into a house on Ferry Street in Malden, seeking escape from what she considered Concord's dull, staid ways.[388] In Concord, the Robinsons had been acquainted with the Alcotts, Channings, Thoreaus and others in Concord's literary circles.[389] William Robinson was a newspaper columnist, frequently out of work, and the family was on hard times when it moved to Malden. By 1866, the family's prospects had improved, and it moved into a house on Lincoln Street, supported by William's job as clerk with the Massachusetts House of Representatives.[390]

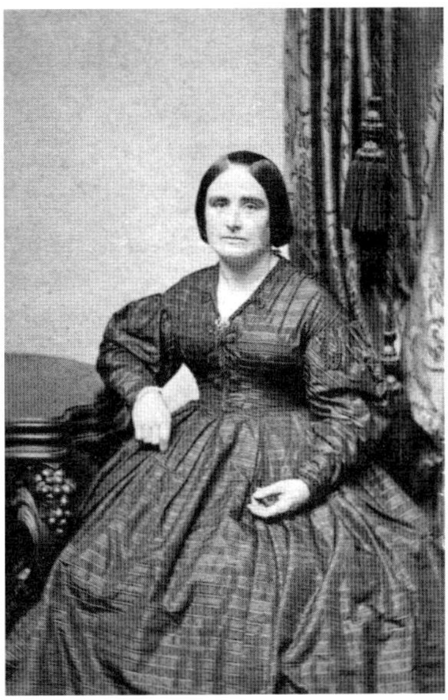

Malden's Harriet Hanson Robinson was a suffragist and reformer. *Malden Historical Society.*

In 1868, Harriet became attracted to the women's suffrage movement after hearing Lucy Stone speak and seeing Julia Ward Howe at the November 1868 New England Convention of the American Equal Rights Association, where was formed the New England Woman Suffrage

Association.[391] Harriet joined the New England association and soon after helped to organize the Middlesex County Woman Suffrage Association and the Malden Woman Suffrage Association.[392] A sample of the attitude the Malden organization would work to change was exhibited when Lucy Stone, a suffragette, first came to Malden. A Universalist minister announced the meeting from the pulpit as such: "This evening, at town hall, a hen will attempt to crow."[393]

In 1875, the Middlesex County Woman Suffrage Association sponsored a convention in Malden. Speeches were given by Julia Ward Howe, Lucy Stone, Harriet Robinson and others. Letters were received from William Lloyd Garrison, Elizur Wright and Bishop Gilbert Haven.[394] Resolutions were adopted by the Malden Convention, as follows:

> *Resolved, That Woman has an equal right with man to the ballot, and that to deprive her of the use of it is an act of usurpation which ought to be immediately discontinued.*
>
> *Resolved, That we care not whether the right of Suffrage be called natural and absolute, or conventional, or dependent on capacity, or property, or on any kind of qualification which may be acquired, it is the same in woman as in man; that historically and legally—by Genesis and by the Statutes, this equality is especially recognized.*
>
> *Resolved, that the Legislature of Massachusetts, be persisting in its opposition to the granting of all petitions for removal of usurping rules and statutes on the subject, is unjust, and that, no matter whether this spirit and practice of injustice be the result of carelessness or ignorance or malice, it is duty at once to correct it, and no longer to interpose its own will and willfulness against the demand of justice and the dictates of duty.*[395]

Harriet Hanson Robinson's daughter, Harriette Lucy Robinson, also became active in the suffrage movement. For ten years, Harriette was president of the National Woman Suffrage Movement in Massachusetts. After a brief period in Nebraska, Harriette, now married with the surname Shattuck, returned to Malden. She was published in the *North American Review* and was correspondent for the *Boston Journal*, *Boston Daily Advertiser* and the *Malden City Press*. She reported on the Concord Summer Schools of Philosophy between 1881 and 1887 for the *Boston Transcript* and wrote several children's books.[396]

Both Harriet Hanson Robinson and her daughter, Harriette, were members of an early Boston women's club, the New England Woman's Club, founded

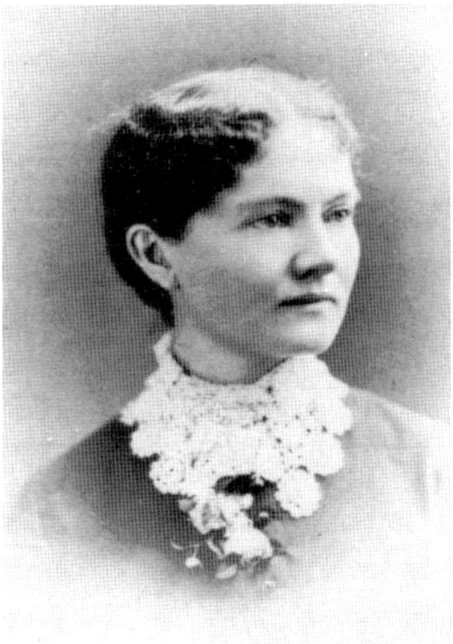

Anna Christy Fall, wife of Mayor George Howard Fall, was the first woman to try a case before a jury in Massachusetts and argue before the Massachusetts Supreme Judicial Court. *Malden Historical Society.*

in 1869. At the time, women's clubs were looked on with disfavor by many men. The younger Robinson attended a congress in New York in 1878, sponsored by the Association for the Advancement of Women, which encouraged the formation of women's clubs. Filled with zeal after this conference, Harriette set about to organize a woman's club in Malden. In 1878, she and thirteen friends met at the home of her mother, Harriet Hanson Robinson, and organized the Old and New, Malden's earliest women's organization.[397] The following year, 1879, Massachusetts allowed women the right to vote for school committee, and Harriette was the first woman registered to vote in the state.[398] Soon thereafter, Emily G. Freeman was elected to the Malden School Committee by the town meeting—the first woman to hold elective office in Malden.[399] In about 1893, the Enterprise Club was formed by working women and girls to secure greater opportunities for advancement.[400] Harriet Robinson died in 1911, and her daughter continued to reside on Lincoln Street until her death in 1926.

Anna Christy Fall was one of the first female lawyers in Massachusetts. Married to George Howard Fall, a one-time mayor of Malden, Anna was the first woman to try a case before a jury in Massachusetts and the first woman to argue a case before the Supreme Judicial Court. She was responsible in large measure for reform of estate administration statutes, which then favored men. Her paper read before the Old and New, entitled "The Tragedy of a Widow's Third," was later published and distributed to the General Court in aid of her reform efforts.[401]

Malden residents were also, in some cases, progressive in politics, mirroring a rise in progressivism and populism among farmers and laborers.[402] In 1893, a bitter municipal election pitted the Republican, James Pierce, against Major Henry Winn, an Independent, for mayor.[403] Pierce had frequently been chosen moderator of the town meeting in the old town days and was a prominent political figure. Winn was a socialist aligned with Edward Bellamy

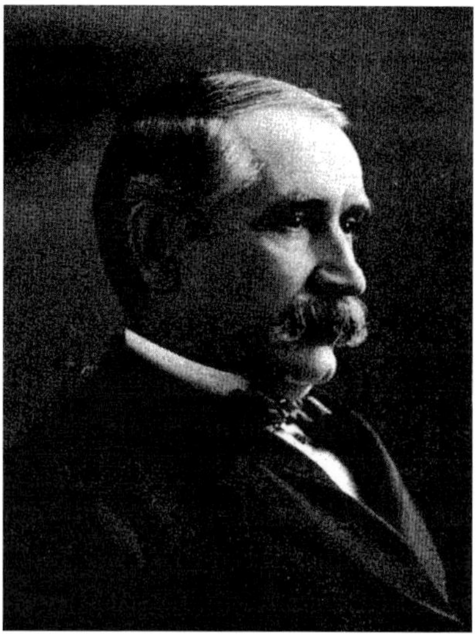

Henry Winn, the socialist mayor of Malden in 1893. *Malden Historical Society*.

and the nascent Nationalist Party. He had run for governor in 1891 under the banner of the New People's Party. Falling short of the mark, Winn ran for mayor in 1892, though on several occasions, if hostile newspaper accounts can be believed, Winn was overheard to say he knew little about city affairs or administration. "The intelligent people of Malden have tried Mayor Pierce for one year and are entirely satisfied with him," assured the pro-Republican, pro-Pierce *Malden Mirror* in a page-one article just before the election. Further, "the almost unknown candidate who has been nominated for the mayoralty by the 'independent committee' deserves to be relegated to retirement....The candidate has no knowledge whatever of the duties incumbent upon the Mayor of Malden." Lest readers miss the point, the *Mirror* inserted here and there throughout its edition, in large bold type, the admonition: "Don't vote for a crank...Vote for Hon. James Pierce for Mayor."[404] Conversely, Bellamy's newspaper, the *New Nation*, touted the progressive, trust-busting nature of Winn: "If it is the purpose of the citizens of Malden to choose a local executive who has had a life training in limiting the sway of rings and advocating clean and honest methods of administration, we are confident that they will make no mistake in seeking to gain their ends by the election of Henry Winn."[405]

Winn won the mayoralty, 2,115 to 1,725, and his Independents took a majority of the board of aldermen and common council. Progressives in Massachusetts took note of the election of a socialist mayor: "The election of Maj. Henry Winn...as mayor of the wealthy and intelligent city of Malden, may well be regarded as one of the most significant events of the time. It shows that though the people are not yet ready for very radical measures...a man who advocates them is no longer necessarily regarded as being either a fool, crank, or villain."[406]

Edward Bellamy, the nationalist movement and its Malden connection deserve some brief attention. In 1888, Edward Bellamy authored a utopian novel called *Looking Backward* for which Sylvester Baxter later penned an introduction.[407] Owing to the novel's popularity, Bellamy clubs began to spring up nationwide and led to a movement called the nationalist movement, which was loosely aligned with socialism, although nationalists sought to differentiate themselves from socialism.[408] Baxter was a proponent of the nationalist movement and, in fact, founded the first nationalist club in Boston.[409] The movement largely channeled middle-class discontent with economic issues.

Around the same time, a religious utopian movement called theosophy was in ascendance. An international Theosophical Society was begun in 1883 by Madame Blavatsky. Soon thereafter in 1886 a Malden Theosophical Society was founded with Baxter at the helm, George David Ayers as vice-president and Frank Shipley Collins as secretary.[410] The utopian nature of Bellamy's *Looking Backward* appealed to the theosophists. For a while, many theosophists joined nationalist clubs. However the nationalist clubs began to orient themselves with the socialist-inspired People's Party. Thus, the theosophists were forced to choose between the National Party and the theosophical society, which opposed associating with political movements. Baxter, Ayers and other theosophists began to move away from Bellamy. Soon thereafter, the nationalist movement died, to be absorbed by the People's Party and the socialists.[411]

Chapter 13

MALDEN AT THE END OF THE NINETEENTH CENTURY

With the increased, rapid growth of Malden, new social organizations came into being. The Malden Club was prominent in the town but failed to satisfy a growing need among businessmen and their families for a place of recreation and social acquaintance.[412] One of the more popular clubs, the Kernwood Club, was organized in 1889 for "social and literary purposes." The club soon attracted many of Malden's prominent citizens as members, purchased land on Alpine Street and erected a clubhouse with views overlooking the city.[413] The club's opening was a glittering, formal affair: Chinese lanterns illuminated the clubhouse and hung in the windows and on trees, and the inside was lit with electric light and decorated with palms, garlands and chrysanthemums. Guests arrived at eight o'clock and danced to Carter's band until one o'clock in the morning.[414] During its life, the club entertained the likes of William Howard Taft, Henry Cabot Lodge, Jimmy Foxx and Ted Williams.[415] Bowling, amateur theatricals and vaudeville entertainments were social events.[416] The club flourished until the 1950s, when, like similar neighborhood clubs in other cities, it became less popular and disbanded.

The Deliberative Assembly was a debating organization organized in 1875. It later evolved into the Ex-Aldermen's Club, the criteria for membership having been elected to serve in the city government. Its annual Crow Supper was a popular political roast until the 1980s. It was an unspoken assumption that the "better" classes of Malden men followed a social circle that began in the high school with membership in the Literary

Society. After graduation, young men of means would join the Deliberative Assembly and the Kernwood or Malden Clubs.[417] The more effete would join the University Club, which sponsored talks by academics and learned persons. The Malden Historical Society was established in 1886 to collect and preserve the rapidly disappearing history of Malden.

Service organization also sprang up. One of the earliest was the Ladies' Aid Association of the Malden Hospital, organized in 1892 by a group of women representing the various churches in Malden to raise awareness and funds for the new hospital. The Malden Hospital itself was opened in 1892 on land donated by Elisha Converse for that purpose. In September 1891, a group of business and civic leaders organized the Malden Board of Trade (today's chamber of commerce). The Malden Young Men's Christian Association formed in the 1880s to enrich the spirits, minds and bodies of its members.

Leisure time became available. The Pine Banks Golf Club attracted Malden society to its links.[418] The Maplewood Gun Club had a clubhouse off Granite Street. Sylvester Baxter began the Middlesex Bicycle Club as early as 1882.[419] In fact, Malden was a hub for bicycle races in the 1880s and 1890s and caught the bicycling craze. Most popular were the annual Linscott Road Races. Races were run down Eastern Avenue from Jim Linscott's bicycle shop to places as far away as Belmont and Waltham. Other races went through Maplewood and Linden. Crowds thronged the sidewalks to watch Malden's champion racer, Eddie McDuffee. The Linscott race of 1895 in particular attracted thousands to Malden. Among the racers was young Alvan "Allie" Fuller, later to become governor of the commonwealth. Fuller opened a bicycle shop on Cross Street near the Belmont school and parlayed that into becoming Boston's first and largest automobile dealer, by which he amassed a fortune.[420] Maggie Kirkwood of Maplewood was a famous female bicycle racer.[421]

Football and baseball became popular. Malden had a town baseball team, the Pequod Base Ball Club, as early as 1866. The *Boston Journal* reported in 1867 on a game between the "Washingtons" of Malden Centre and the Atalanta Base Ball Club of South Malden. By 1878, the Malden Base Ball Club had become established. Thousands would watch games at Ferryway Green.[422] Football came to Malden at the high school in 1889. It soon replaced the old military drill. In 1894, the school newspaper, *The Oracle*, reported that "since drill has been abandoned, athletics must take a prominent place among the functions of our school."[423] Malden's annual football rivalry with Medford began on October 15, 1889; Malden lost 30–0. The game was moved to Thanksgiving Day in 1899. It is the fifth-oldest continuous high school football rivalry in the nation.[424] Other diversions were skating, sledding, track and field events and ice polo, an early ancestor of ice hockey.[425]

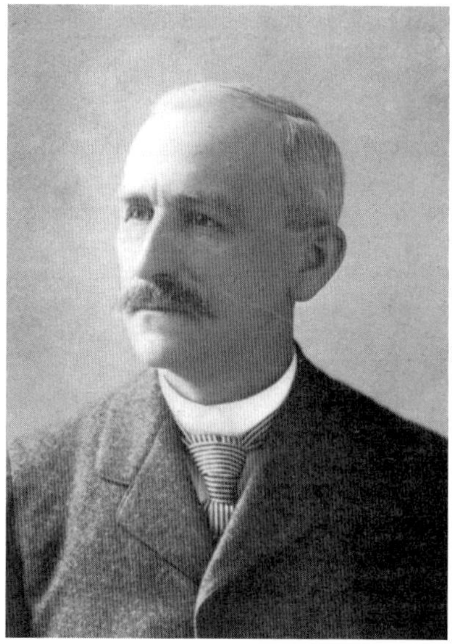

James Bailey Upham was editor of the *Youth's Companion* and the author of the Pledge of Allegiance. He lived on Lincoln Street. *Malden Historical Society.*

One of the most popular children's magazines at the time was the *Youth's Companion*. Its publisher was Daniel Ford. Ford brought on his nephew, James Bailey Upham, as a business partner. Upham resided on Lincoln Street, a few doors down from Harriet Hanson Robinson. He was a member of the First Baptist Church and Converse Masonic Lodge. Upham devised a promotion to distribute an American flag to every public school in the country and have students recite an oath to the flag in connection with the 400th anniversary of Columbus's discovery of America.[426] Its recitation was to be accompanied with a raised arm salute and upturned hand. Upham came up with a rough draft of the pledge, circulating it among staff for comments and changes. Among those was Francis Bellamy, cousin of Edward Bellamy and a socialist. When the Pledge of Allegiance was first printed in the *Youth's Companion* on September 8, 1892, in connection with the official program of the 1892 Columbus Day celebration, it was called the "*Youth's Companion* Pledge of Allegiance," with no attribution to its authorship. The magazine apparently had a non-attribution policy.[427] The original text of the Pledge was published, as follows: "I pledge allegiance to my Flag and the Republic for which it stands: one nation indivisible, with liberty and Justice for all."[428] Upham was present in Malden on that Columbus Day in 1892 and heard the Pledge recited by more than 1,500 adults at a mass meeting.[429]

The magazine maintained until the 1920s that Upham was the author of the Pledge. Indeed, it published a story touting Upham's authorship in 1917 in response to an inquiry from Herbert Fison, the librarian in Malden. Bellamy was apparently furious and over a period of several years asserted that he was the author. The controversy between Upham and Bellamy simmered for several years before boiling over. Margarette

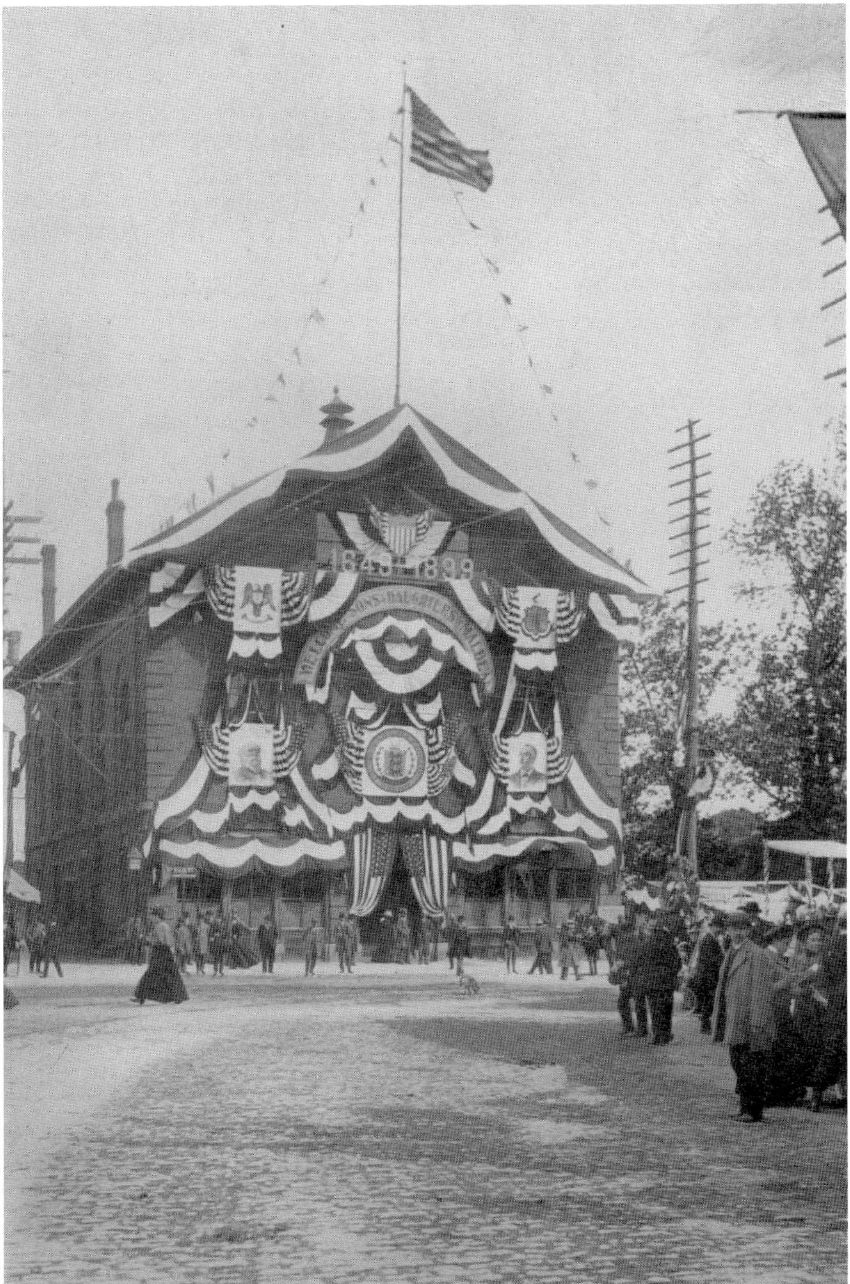

Malden City Hall is seen decorated for Malden's 250th anniversary in May 1899. *Author's collection.*

Miller, in *Twenty-Three Words*, maintained that it was Bellamy.[430] The late David Brickman, editor at the *Malden Evening News*, and reporter Archie Birtwell gathered evidence and affidavits to establish Upham's claim.[431] The Massachusetts legislature declared Upham the author.[432] The Library of Congress weighed in and declared Bellamy the author.[433] Today, most references credit Upham as giving genesis to the idea of the pledge and Bellamy with its writing. Not this one. We in Malden know better and stand with Brickman and Birtwell: James Bailey Upham authored the Pledge of Allegiance.

Malden celebrated its 250th anniversary in grand style and invited all of Massachusetts, especially the press, to the party. Houses were decorated with flags and pictures of President McKinley.[434] From May 20 to 23, 1899, Malden celebrated on a grand scale with a huge parade, banquet, formal ball, field and athletic contests, a minstrel show, literary exercises and an exhibition of historical artifacts. While Malden society may have enjoyed the literary exercises and formal ball and banquet, the mass of the population was more interested in the athletic contests and the fakirs that seemingly filled the city:

> *Fakers and philosophers with long beards and pale faces, peripatetic peddlers with souvenirs and refreshments shrilly crying their wares, hand-organs and monkeys, soap-sellers and toy-vendors…penetrated the crowds in every direction; while the din of firecrackers, large and small, the snap of torpedoes, the hiss of toy balloons, and the dissonant toots of horns were audible evidence of a crowd which was intent upon pleasure. Vacant lots were covered with booths, sheltering stores of pink lemonade and sandwiches, airgun and knife-throwing targets, or some of the many opportunities for refreshment and cheap amusement to which the onlookers were loudly invited.*[435]

A balloon ascension at Ferryway Green attracted thousands, as did fireworks at Eaton's Field (today's Roosevelt Field).[436] Athletic contests included swimming races at Fellsmere Pond, bicycle races, track and field, Gaelic football, baseball and golf.[437]

As the din of the crowd and the smell of the fireworks sulfur faded, Malden could look forward to the new century approaching. Few could foresee the rapid changes that would soon arrive in the twentieth century: the arrival of a large number of Jews after the great Chelsea fire of 1908, which would remake the face of Malden; the opening of the

Converse Rubber Company, Malden's largest employer and nationally famous maker of sneakers for generations; the departure of most wealthy inhabitants to upscale communities; and the sacrifices of Malden men and women in World War I. Yet Malden was prepared to accept these and other changes.

NOTES

Chapter 1

1. Much of the early history of Malden up to 1785 I have condensed from a short article by Deloraine P. Corey that was published in Samuel Adams Drake, *History of Middlesex County, Massachusetts*, vol. 2 (Boston: Estes & Lauriat, 1880), 113–36. Citations to that article are omitted. Readers can refer to that article for more information or, better yet, to Deloraine Corey, *History of Malden, Massachusetts, 1633–1785* (Cambridge, MA: University Press, 1899), which is extensively footnoted to original sources. Where there is a citation, the research is my own. There is also a history of Malden by William T. Davis in D. Hamilton Hurd, ed., *History of Middlesex County, Massachusetts* (Philadelphia: J.W. Lewis, 1890), 456–76. Though of limited value, the Davis material consolidates some reference material not readily found elsewhere, such as a list of Revolutionary War enlistments (page 473) and a list of Malden's representatives in the General Court (page 475).
2. The brook and the river it leads into have had varying historical names. Spot Pond Brook is also sometimes called Three Mile Brook. The Malden River is also referred to as the North River.
3. Letter of George Odiorne in R.H. Eddy, *Report on the Introduction of Soft Water into the City of Boston* (Boston: John H. Eastburn, 1836), 34–35.
4. Quoted in Adrian Tinniswood, *The Rainborowes: One Family's Quest to Build a New England* (New York: Basic Books, 2013), 118.

5. Ibid., 177.
6. Ibid., 191–92. See also Charles Edward Mann, "The Governor's Lady: Why One of Malden's Public Parks Is Called 'Coytemore Lea,'" *Register of the Malden Historical Society*, vol. 6 (Lynn, MA: Frank S. Whitten, 1920), 13, 14–17.
7. Mann, "Governor's Lady."
8. Tinniswood, *Rainborowes*, 287.
9. Ibid., 309.

Chapter 2

10. Deloraine P. Corey, *Joseph Hills and the Massachusetts Laws of 1648* (Boston: William Sanford Hills, 1899).
11. Corey, *History of Malden, Massachusetts*, 146.
12. For a brief overview of Wigglesworth, see Edmund S. Morgan's "The Puritan's Puritan: Michael Wigglesworth" in Edmund S. Morgan, *American Heroes: Profiles of Men and Women Who Shaped Early America* (New York: W.W. Norton, 2009), 102–11. For a full biography, see Richard Crowder, *No Featherbed to Heaven: A Biography of Michael Wigglesworth, 1631–1705* (East Lansing: Michigan State University Press, 1962). An older effort is John Ward Dean, *Memoir of Rev. Michael Wigglesworth*, 2nd ed. (Albany, NY: Joel Munsell, 1871). For Wigglesworth's diary, see Edmund S. Morgan, ed., *The Diary of Michael Wigglesworth, 1653–1657: The Conscience of a Puritan* (Gloucester, MA: Peter Smith, 1951). The quotation is taken from the inscription on Wigglesworth's headstone in Bell Rock Cemetery.
13. Cotton Mather, *A Faithful Man Described and Rewarded: A Sermon Preached at Maldon on June 24, 1705, Occasioned by the Departure of that Faithful and Aged Servant of God; Mr. Michael Wigglesworth* (Boston: J. Putham, 1849). This 1849 imprint erroneously credits Increase Mather as the author. Increase Mather wrote the introduction; Cotton Mather preached the funeral sermon.
14. Harvell's Brook later became the Saugus Branch Creek and exists today in an underground culvert that runs beneath the Northern Strand Bicycle Trail. Cross Street was called Harvell's Brook Lane in that vicinity.
15. Roger Thompson, *Sex in Middlesex: Popular Mores in a Massachusetts County, 1649–1699* (Amherst: University of Massachusetts Press, 1986), 14.
16. Ibid., 132–33.
17. Ibid., 185.

18. Ibid., 179, n. 71.
19. Jill Lepore, "When Deer Island Was Turned into Devil's Island," *Bostonia: The Alumni Quarterly of Boston University* (Summer 1998): 14; Corey, *History of Malden, Massachusetts*, 46.
20. Thompson, *Sex in Middlesex*, 186, n. 115.
21. For an account of Joseph Emerson, see Phyllis Cole, *Mary Moody Emerson and the Origins of Transcendentalism* (New York: Oxford University Press, 2002), 25–30.
22. See Samuel Eliot Morison and Henry Steele Commager, *The Growth of the American Republic*, vol. 1, 4th ed. (New York: Oxford University Press, 1950), 110–12.
23. Charles Edward Mann, "Methodist Beginnings in Malden," *Register of the Malden Historical Society*, vol. 4 (Lynn, MA: Frank S. Whitten, 1916), 30, 32–36.
24. For a biography, see Cole, *Mary Moody Emerson*. Some of her letters are collected in Nancy Craig Simmons, ed., *The Selected Letters of Mary Moody Emerson* (Athens: University of Georgia Press, 1993). Mary Moody Emerson's "Almanacks" have been digitized, and some are available online at www.marymoodyemerson.net.
25. Cole, *Mary Moody Emerson*, 12. Ralph Waldo Emerson continued to visit the graves of his ancestors of Malden throughout his life. Indeed, there exists a rare photograph of him taken at Eliphalet J. Foss's "Garden Studio" on Florence Street during one of his visits to Malden in 1873.
26. John Dexter was first appointed an ensign of the foot company in Malden by Governor William Shirley in 1743. See Orlando Perry Dexter, *Dexter Genealogy, 1642–1904: Being a History of the Descendants of Richard Dexter of Malden, Massachusetts* (New York: J.J. Little, 1904), 44–45.
27. For a discussion of the four generations of Lamson family stonecutters, see Ralph L. Tucker, "The Lamson Family Gravestone Carvers of Charlestown and Malden," *Markers: The Journal of the Association for Gravestone Studies* 10 (1993): 151–217.
28. Deed of William Waitt to James Dalton, July 29, 1747, in the collection of the Massachusetts Historical Society.
29. Dexter, *Dexter Genealogy*, 45.
30. See *Commonwealth v. Jennison* (1783) in *Proceedings of the Massachusetts Historical Society, 1873–1875* (Boston, 1875), 292–95. The court held that because the Massachusetts Declaration of Rights declared "all men are born free and equal," slavery had been abolished.

Chapter 3

31. Morison and Commager, *Growth of the American Republic*, vol. 1, 149.
32. Ibid., 149–50.
33. Town clerk's minutes of meetings of the board of selectmen in possession of the Malden Public Library.
34. Morison and Commager, *Growth of the American Republic*, vol. 1, 150, 152.
35. Ibid., 153.
36. Henry Steele Commager and Milton Cantor, eds., *Documents of American History*, vol. 1, 10th ed. (Englewood Cliffs, NJ: Prentice Hall, 1988), 67–68.
37. *Boston Evening Post*, April 9, 1770, 4.
38. Helen Tilden Wild, *Medford in the Revolution* (Medford, MA: J.C. Miller Jr., 1903), 5.
39. *Boston Gazette*, October 3, 1774, 1.
40. The towns were Boston, Roxbury, Dorchester, Watertown, Charlestown, Cambridge, Mistick, Dedham, Milton, Malden, Braintree, Woburn and Stow.
41. Peter Force, *American Archives*, series 4, vol. 1 (Washington, D.C.: Peter Force, 1837), 807–8.
42. Letter of Captain John Dexter, chairman of joint Committee of Correspondence of Malden and Chelsea, May 8, 1775, in Force, *American Archives*, series 4, vol. 2, 536. One omission in Corey's *History of Malden* is the absence of a discussion of Malden's Loyalists. A full understanding of Malden during the Revolution is incomplete without one. I have searched in vain. There is no mention of Malden in James Stark, *The Loyalists of Massachusetts and the Other Side of the American Revolution* (Boston: W.B. Clarke, 1910). To be sure, there must have been Loyalists in Malden. This is fertile ground for an enterprising researcher. Danforth resided in Chelsea. Though a Loyalist, he apparently remained in Chelsea throughout the Revolution. Ironically, he engaged in several land transactions with Benjamin Blaney after the Revolution. See Mellen Chamberlain, *A Documentary History of Chelsea* (Boston: Massachusetts Historical Society, 1908), 317, n. 13, 387–90. One Henry Gardner was a Loyalist in Salem who lived his later life in Malden. See Frank A. Gardner, "Thomas Gardner, Planter and Some of His Descendants," *Essex Institute Historical Collections*, vol. 39 (Salem, MA: Essex Institute, January 1903), 349–52.
43. Peter Thacher, Benjamin Blaney and Elisha Story, Malden Committee of Correspondence and Inspection to Committee of Safety, May 25, 1775, in Force, *American Archives*, series 4, vol. 2, 708.

44. Letter of Colonel Loammi Baldwin concerning three women from Boston, August 5, 1775, in Force, *American Archives*, series 4, vol. 3, 312.
45. Ibid. See also J.L. Bell, *George Washington's Headquarters and Home—Cambridge, Massachusetts, Historic Resource Study* (Washington, D.C.: National Park Service, 2012), 416.
46. Information of Eldad Taylor, December 4, 1775, in Force, *American Archives*, series 4, vol. 4, 1,321.
47. Letter from Thomas Crafts to George Washington, December 10, 1775, in Force, *American Archives*, series 4, vol. 4, 1,229. See also letter from Thomas Crafts to William Cooper, December 10, 1775, in Force, *American Archives*, series 4, vol. 4, 1,229.
48. Dudley P. Bailey, "Everett: A Historical Sketch," in *Everett Souvenir* (Everett, MA: Everett Souvenir Company, 1893), 10.
49. Wild, *Medford in the Revolution*, 8; S. Osgood Wright, *An Historical Discourse Delivered at Malden, Mass. on the Day of the Annual Thanksgiving, December 1, 1831* (Boston: Lyceum Press, Light and Harris, 1832), 20.
50. David Hackett Fischer, *Paul Revere's Ride* (New York: Oxford University Press, 1994), 140–41.
51. Ibid., 251.
52. Also called Beacham's Point or, in later years, Wormwood Point or VanVoorhis Point. It was located near the end of Beacham Street at a point on the Island End River.
53. Wright, *Historical Discourse*, 20.
54. Also called the Battle of Noddle's Island.
55. Thacher's narrative is reproduced in Henry Steele Commager and Richard B. Morris, eds., *The Spirit of 'Seventy-Six: The Story of the American Revolution as Told by Participants* (New York: Harper & Row, 1967), 126–28.
56. Ibid., 121.
57. *Analectic Magazine* 11 (March 1818): 257.
58. Wright, *Historical Discourse*, 21.
59. Wild, *Medford in the Revolution*, 24.
60. Ibid., 12–13.
61. Is the legend true? Perhaps. It was reported in the *Bunker Hill Aurora* on April 16, 1853, by Richard Dexter, who supposedly witnessed the incident when he was nineteen. See Dexter, *Dexter Genealogy*, 46–47.
62. Peter Thacher, "Oration Delivered at Watertown, March 5, 1776," *Boston Orations* (Boston: Peter Edes, 1785), 73–83
63. Ibid., 73–83, excerpts.

64. Pauline Maier, *American Scripture: The Making of the Declaration of Independence* (New York: Alfred A. Knopf, 1997), 59.
65. Ibid., 220. The distinction of being the first town to declare for independence goes to Chelmsford, Massachusetts, which passed resolutions on May 13, 1776. Nine other Massachusetts towns passed resolutions before Malden acted. See the excellent discussion of Malden's instructions and those of other localities in Maier's chapter entitled "The Other Declarations of Independence," 59–90.
66. Corey, *History of Malden, Massachusetts*, 765.
67. Commager and Morris, *Spirit of 'Seventy-Six*, 297–98. Commager and Morris take their text from that copy in the Massachusetts Archives. This version omits the final paragraph. A slightly different version, taken from the town clerk's record book, is reproduced in Corey, *History of Malden, Massachusetts*, 762–64, from which I have added the final paragraph. See also Hezekiah Niles, *Principles and Acts of the Revolution in America* (Baltimore, MD: William Ogden Niles, 1822), 156–57. The version in Niles is also contained in Commager and Cantor, *Documents of American History*, vol. 1, 96–98. The Malden instructions are also reproduced in Force, *American Archives*, series 4, vol. 6, 602–3.
68. See *An Act to Incorporate a Society, by the Name of the Massachusetts Historical Society* (St. 1793, c. 36). Thacher's diaries from 1764 to 1799 are in the collection of the Massachusetts Historical Society.
69. William Emerson, *A Sermon on the Decease of the Rev. Peter Thacher* (Boston: Young & Minns, 1803).
70. Force, *American Archives*, series 5, vol. 1, 460–61.

Chapter 4

71. There is much literature on the missionary Adoniram Judson, and a review of his life is beyond the scope of this brief history. Those interested would do well to begin with the standard biography: Courtney Anderson, *To the Golden Shore: The Life of Adoniram Judson* (Boston: Little, Brown & Company, 1956).
72. George Walter Chamberlain, "The Early Baptists of Malden," *Register of the Malden Historical Society*, vol. 5 (Lynn, MA: Frank S. Whitten, 1918), 13.
73. Deloraine P. Corey, "A Walk Up Salem Street," *Register of the Malden Historical Society*, vol. 5 (Lynn, MA: Frank S. Whitten, 1918), 5, 6–7.

74. The James Howard House still stands, much altered, as a private home at 24–28 Holm Court.
75. Paul Revere, "Memorandum of Bells, 1801–1810," in the collection of Massachusetts Historical Society.
76. Timothy Dexter was born in Malden. For a biography, see John P. Marquand, *Lord Timothy Dexter of Newburyport, Massachusetts: First in the East, First in the West, and the Greatest Philosopher in the Western World* (New York: Milton, Balch & Company, 1925), or John P. Marquand, *Timothy Dexter, Revisited* (Boston: Little, Brown & Company, 1960). See also Samuel L. Knapp, *Life of Lord Timothy Dexter* (Boston: J.E. Tilton, 1858), and Dexter, *Dexter Genealogy*, 78–82.
77. Deloraine P. Corey, "The Old Brick," *Register of the Malden Historical Society*, vol. 6 (Lynn, MA: Frank S. Whitten, 1920), 5.
78. Marquand, *Lord Timothy Dexter*, 14 (spelling is Dexter's).
79. Ibid., 54–59.
80. Ibid., 200.
81. Ibid., 254–61. The mansion still exists; the statues are long gone.
82. Ibid., 240–42.
83. Timothy Dexter, *A Pickle for the Knowing Ones*, reproduced in Knapp, *Life of Lord Timothy Dexter*, 123–53. Copies of *Pickle* are still printed by the Newburyport Historical Society.
84. Dexter, *Dexter Genealogy*, 79–80. The will is reproduced in Knapp, *Life of Lord Timothy Dexter*, 154–57.
85. For a general history, see J. Russell Bowman and Edward B. Seeley, *A Short History of First Parish in Malden 1649–1974 and of the First Parish in Malden, Universalist, 1828–1974* (Malden, MA: First Parish in Malden, Universalist, 1974).
86. Those interested in early church history in Malden should consult Joshua W. Wellman, "Ecclesiastical History of Malden," in Hurd, *History of Middlesex County*, vol. 3, 477–526. See also J.G. Adams, "Historical Sketch of the First Parish in Malden," *Universalist Miscellany* 6, no. 5 (November 1848): 168–75.
87. Charles Brooks and James Usher, *History of the Town of Medford* (Boston: Rand, Avery & Company, 1886; reprint, Franklin Press, 1975), 87.
88. Reverend David Osgood, June 28, 1786, reprinted in Brooks and Usher, *History of the Town of Medford*, 87–89. The entire letter is reproduced in Brooks and Usher's work.
89. Brooks and Usher, *History of the Town of Medford*, 87.

90. Joseph E. Garland, *Boston's North Shore* (Boston: Little, Brown & Company, 1978) 5.
91. George A. Kyle, *The Straight Road: A Short Account of the Newburyport Turnpike and Early Days in Everett, Massachusetts* (Everett, MA: Everett National Bank, 1927), 5.
92. *Malden Bridge to the People* (Boston, MA, 1829).
93. Portions of this road today are known as Lynn Street, School Street and Broadway. Kyle, *Straight Road*, 4.
94. Today the Newburyport Turnpike is called Broadway in Malden and Everett.
95. Kyle, *Straight Road*, 15–16. See also Nathan Mortimer Hawkes, "Milestone Memorials Along Newburyport Turnpike," *Register of the Lynn Historical Society*, vol. 17 (Lynn, MA: Frank S. Whitten, 1914), 123–51. The turnpike was originally to have terminated at Chelsea Bridge. Hawkes, "Milestone Memorials Along Newburyport Turnpike," 125.
96. Kyle, *Straight Road*, 20–22.
97. Henry C. Binford in his study of early suburbs on the Boston periphery noted three stages of suburban development in the early suburbs. First, from the Federalist era to the depression of 1837–43: the growth of manufactures and commercial activity related to Boston but not requiring constant contact. The second stage was from the 1830s to the 1850s: suburbanites promoted roads, bridges, omnibuses and rail lines, triggering a revolution in mobility to and from Boston and transforming expectations about work, residence, shopping and government. The third stage came in the 1860s: communities "confidently and articulately defined their communities' role in the Boston metropolis." Malden's development mirrored these three stages. Henry C. Binford, *The First Suburbs: Residential Communities on the Boston Periphery, 1815–1860* (Chicago: University of Chicago Press, 1985), 10.
98. See Linda Thorsen, "The Merchant's Manufacturer: The Barrett Family's Dyeing Business in Massachusetts and New York, 1790–1850," Master's thesis, Harvard University Extension, Cambridge, MA, 2015.
99. *The Bi-Centennial Book of Malden* (Boston: Geo. C. Rand & Company, 1850), 178. Barrett apparently erected a small mill at Spot Pond near the present corner of Pond Street and the Fellsway in an area that would become known as Haywardville. Parker W. Perry, "The Vanished Village of the Fells," *Round About Middlesex Fells* (Medford: Medford Historical Society, 1935), 37, 40. Barrett's son sold this mill, the land and another lot to Elisha S. Converse in the 1840s.

100. Indenture dated March 18, 1804, in the collection of the Boston Public Library, found in "Boston (Mass.) Overseers of the Poor Indentures, 1734–1805," Box 12, Folder 1210. A digital image is available at http://ark.digitalcommonwealth.org/ark./50959/p5548484b.

101. James Creighton Odiorne, *Genealogy of the Odiorne Family* (Boston: Rand, Avery & Company, 1875), 75; letter of George Odiorne in Eddy, *Report on the Introduction of Soft Water*, 34–35. The history of the land titles and uses of Spot Pond and the Spot Pond Brook are extensively explored in a legal brief associated with the commonwealth's taking of Spot Pond for public water supply purposes. See the "Brief of Petitioners" in *City of Malden, et al., Petitioners v. Commonwealth* (Boston: George H. Ellis, 1905), 1–113. See also Douglas L. Heath and Alison C. Simcox, *The Lost Mill Village of Middlesex Fells* (Charleston, SC: The History Press, 2017).

102. John Leander Bishop, Edwin Troxell Freedley and Edward Young, *A History of American Manufactures from 1608 to 1860*, vol. 2 (Philadelphia: Edward Young & Company, 1864), 126, n. 1.

103. *An Act to Incorporate Sundry Persons by the Name of the Malden Nail Manufactory* (St. 1810, c. 74).

104. Orra L. Stone, *History of Massachusetts Industries*, vol. 1 (Boston: S.J. Clarke Publishing Company, 1930), 36–37; William H. Winship, "History of Malden Industries," mss in possession of the Malden Historical Society, 25.

105. James W. Swank, *History of the Manufacture of Iron in All Ages* (Philadelphia: American Iron and Steel Association, 1892), 133.

106. *Boston Directory* (Boston: John H.A. Frost, 1823), 174.

107. Anthony F.C. Wallace, *Rockdale: The Growth of an American Village in the Early Industrial Revolution*, (Lincoln: University of Nebraska Press, 2005), 208; Bishop, Freedley and Young, *History of American Manufactures*, 126, n. 1. See also unsigned letter from one of the Odiorne brothers in *Philadelphia Repertory* 1, no. 9 (June 30, 1810): 71–72.

108. Bishop, Freedley and Young, *History of American Manufactures*, 126, n. 1; *Philadelphia Repertory* 1, no. 9 (June 30, 1810): 71–72.

109. Swank, *History of the Manufacture of Iron*, 448.

110. Thomas Odiorne, *The Progress of Refinement, A Poem in Three Books. To Which Is Added a Poem of Fame and Miscellanies* (Boston: Young and Etheridge, 1792).

111. Binford, *First Suburbs*, 39. For a list of some Malden brickmakers, see invoice for building the meetinghouse in 1803 in Walter Kendall Watkins, "Malden's Old Meetinghouses," *Register of the Malden Historical Society*, vol. 2 (Lynn, MA: Frank S. Whitten, 1912), 33, 51–52.

112. United States Census, 1820, online from familysearch.org.
113. For a thorough discussion of the trial and its implications for equal rights in the early republic, see Richard D. Brown, "'No Harm to Kill Indians': Equal Rights in a Time of War," *New England Quarterly* 81, no. 1 (March 2008): 34–62.
114. *The Trial of Alpheus Livermore and Samuel Angier* (Boston: Watson & Bangs, 1813), 8 and 26.
115. It is unclear to me whether the Odiornes owned the land rights around the pond. Certainly they owned the riparian rights and the rights up to the high-water mark in the pond.
116. Citations to the articles in the Boston press are found in Brown, "No Harm to Kill Indians," 37–38, n. 11–13.
117. *Trial of Alpheus Livermore and Samuel Angier*. The two broadsides are in the collection of the American Antiquarian Society and may be viewed online.
118. Brown, "No Harm to Kill Indians," 47, 49–50.
119. Ibid., 53.
120. Ibid., 58–59.
121. Ibid., 53.
122. Samuel Gardner Drake, *Biography and History of the Indians of North America, from Its First Discovery*, 10th ed. (Boston: Benjamin B. Mussey, 1848), 136–37; William Durkee Williamson, *The History of the State of Maine From Its First Discovery, A.D. 1602, to the Separation, A.D. 1820, Inclusive*, vol. 1 (Hallowell, ME: Glazier, Masters & Smith, 1838), 502.
123. Silas Dean, *A Brief History of the Town of Stoneham: From Its First Settlement to the Year 1843* (Stoneham, MA: Sentinel Press, 1870), 30.
124. J.B. Kerfoot, *American Pewter* (New York: Crown, 1942), 153.
125. Winship, "History of Malden Industries," 28; Timothy Bailey, "Sketch of the Life of Timothy Bailey of Malden," in *Account of the Tenth Gathering of the Bailey—Bayley Family Association* (Boston: Addison C. Getchell & Son, 1905), 55, 61.
126. See for example *An Act to Further Regulate the Shad and Alewife Fishery in the Town of Malden* (St. 1829, c. 129), *An Act to Prevent the Destruction of Oysters & Other Shell Fish in This Commonwealth* (St. 1795, c. 71) and *An Act to Extend the Protections of Shad and Alewife in the Mystic River to Malden* (St. 1793, c. 66).
127. *Cold Storage and Ice Trade Journal* (May 1905): 50.
128. Winship, "History of Malden Industries," 34; Harold H. Harding, "History of Banking in Malden," *Register of the Malden Historical Society*,

vol. 7 (1967), 50, 52; *Boston Banker* 15, no. 2, "History of Malden's Oldest Bank" (December 1941): 2–3.

129. *Sprague v. Waite*, 17 Pick. 309 (1835); Arthur J. Plummer, "Talk to Malden Historical Society," *Register of the Malden Historical Society*, vol. 7 (1967), 50, 55.

130. *An Act to Establish a Fire Department in the Town of Malden* (St. 1839, c. 55).

Chapter 5

131. Edgeworth, Malden Center and Oak Grove.

132. Bell Rock, Malden Center, Faulkner, Maplewood, Broadway and Linden.

133. *Bi-Centennial Book of Malden*, 225.

134. Ibid., 224.

135. *An Act to Incorporate the Edgeworth Company* (St. 1849, c. 190).

136. *Bi-Centennial Book of Malden*, 225.

137. Ibid., 104.

138. *An Act to Establish the Malden Canal Company* (St. 1846, c. 229).

139. J.D. VanSlyck, *New England Manufacturers and Manufactories*, vol. 1 (Boston: VanSlyck and Company, 1879), 119–20.

140. Ibid., 120.

141. The story of Nathaniel Hayward and his race against Charles Goodyear and the lost village of Haywardville, while fascinating, are beyond the scope of this history. An excellent version of the story is presented in Perry, "Vanished Village of the Fells," 37–44. See also Heath and Simcox, *Lost Mill Village of Middlesex Fells*.

142. Letter from E.S. Converse to Gardiner G. Hubbard, July 7, 1877, in Library of Congress, MSS51268, "The American Bell Telephone Company, 1877–1880" folder. A digital image may be seen at http://hdl.loc.gov/loc.mss/magbell.27100102.

143. Charles Allen Converse, ed., *Some of the Ancestors and Descendants of Samuel Converse, Jr.*, vol. 1 (Boston: Eben Putnam, 1905), 60.

144. H.E. Sawyer, *Histories of the United States Rubber Company and Some Subsidiary Companies* ([New York?]: United States Rubber Company, 1916), 12; Stone, *History of Massachusetts Industries*, 908–9. Converse's Boston Rubber Shoe Company should not be confused with the Converse Rubber Company of sneaker fame, which was founded in Malden in 1908 by Marquis M. Converse.

145. Ibid., 13.
146. Ibid., 12.
147. Ibid.
148. VanSlyck, *New England Manufacturers and Manufactories*, 120–24.
149. William G. Hill, *Family Record of Deacons James W. Converse and Elisha Converse* (privately printed, 1887) 183.
150. Ibid., 183.
151. Sawyer, *Histories of the United States Rubber Company*, 13–14.
152. Ibid., 14.
153. Quoted in John A. Garraty, *Henry Cabot Lodge* (New York: Alfred A. Knopf, 1953), 68.
154. Hill, *Family Record of Deacons*, 174–76.
155. Garraty, *Henry Cabot Lodge*, 67–68.
156. *Memorial of the Celebration of the Two Hundred and Fiftieth Anniversary of the Incorporation of the Town of Malden, May, 1899* (Cambridge, MA: University Press, 1900), 266–67.
157. The hall is named for Converse's brother, James W. Converse. Converse, *Some of the Ancestors and Descendants*, 55–56.
158. Converse, *Some of the Ancestors and Descendants*, 58–61.
159. *Commemorating 70 Years of Cuticura, 1878–1948* (Malden, MA: Potter Drug & Chemical Corporation, 1948), n.p.
160. *Malden Past and Present*, 96 (Malden, MA: Malden Mirror, 1899).
161. *Commemorating 70 Years of Cuticura*, n.p. George Robert White became one of Boston's most generous philanthropists, giving large amounts to the Massachusetts General Hospital, Massachusetts College of Pharmacy and the Museum of Fine Arts. Upon his death, he left $5.5 million in trust to the City of Boston. A memorial to him stands in Boston's Public Garden. Although he was born in Lynnfield and resided in Boston and Manchester-by-the-Sea, White undoubtedly came to the Malden factory and therefore his association with the city is worthy of note.
162. It has since been converted into apartments known as the Robinson-Cuticura apartments.
163. Marion R. Cummings, "Malden Horse Car Days," *Register of the Malden Historical Society*, vol. 7, 21.
164. The church, in its present location, was then located in Medford. An act of the legislature later added the land to Malden. Brooks and Usher, *History of the Town of Medford*, 278.
165. *In Memory of Elisha Slade Converse* (Malden, MA: City of Malden, 1905), 11–12.

166. Louise F. Hunt, "The Roman Catholic Church in Medford," *Medford Historical Register* 17, no. 1 (January 1914): 1–4; James S. Sullivan, ed., *One Hundred Years of Progress: A Graphic, Historical and Pictorial Account of the Catholic Church of New England: Archdiocese of Boston* (Boston: Illustrated Publishing Company, 1895), 584; Reverend Mark V. Carr, "Immaculate Conception Plans Centenary," mss in possession of Malden Historical Society (1955).
167. Personal communication with the late Charles D. Kelley and attorney Charles D. Kelley Jr.
168. The cemetery, long forgotten and vandalized, its history lost, was the focus of a remarkable restoration in 2013 by the Jewish Cemetery Association of Massachusetts. *Jewish Times*, "Forgotten Children Remembered at Historic MA Cemetery," December 24, 2013; *Boston Globe*, "Jewish Cemetery in Malden Restored to Honor Forgotten Souls," October 5, 2013.
169. Avraham (Alfred) Greenbaum, *A Congregational History of Malden Jewry* (Malden, MA: Malden Public Library, 2001), 2.
170. Elliott Paul, *Linden on the Saugus Branch* (New York: Random House, 1947), 263.
171. C. Nelson Bishop, *A Brief Historical Account of the Malden High School Literary Society* (Reading, MA: Reading Chronicle Press, 1947), 8. Bishop said that Jewish boys were admitted before 1915, but after the creation of the Lyceum, they were not. The Lyceum was short-lived and was supplanted by the Cognoscendi Causa Society (COG) in 1922, again primarily Jewish. See also Paul, *Linden on the Saugus Branch*, 269 (discussing segregation among Malden High School fraternities).
172. United States Census, 1800 and 1840, on familysearch.org.
173. *Emmanuel Baptist Church Souvenir Book*, "Historical Sketch of the Union Baptist Church, Malden, Massachusetts" (Malden, MA: Emmanuel Baptist Church, 1996), n.p.
174. Commager and Cantor, *Documents of American History*, vol. 1, 559–61.
175. Wing-kai To and Chinese Historical Society of New England, *Chinese in Boston, 1870–1965* (Charleston, SC: Arcadia Publishing, 2008), 12.
176. *Autobiography of the First Forty-One Years of the Life of Sylvanus Cobb* (Boston: Universalist Publishing House, 1867), 240.
177. Mildred F. Hall, "History of Malden City Hall," *Register of the Malden Historical Society*, vol. 7 (1967), 6, 9.
178. Wright, *Historical Discourse*, 27.
179. *Medford Historical Register* 13, no. 4 (October 1910): 93–95.

180. But see Kyna Hamill, "Upsotting the 'One Horse Open Sleigh': The Blackface Origin of Jingle Bells," *Medford Historical Society & Museum Newsletter* (Winter 2016).
181. Bruce Gellerman and Erik Sherman, *Boston Curiosities* (Guilford, CT: Globe Pequot Press, 2010), 173.
182. *Malden Messenger* (1856–72), *Malden Mirror* (1870–1914), *Malden City Press* (1880–95), *Malden Evening Mail* (1887–1919) and *Malden Evening News* (1892–2017).
183. *Ninth Report of the Free Public Library Commissioners of Massachusetts* (Boston: Wright & Potter, 1899), 212.
184. *Oration, Poem, Speeches, and Chronicles, etc. at the Dedication of the Malden Town Hall* (Malden, MA: Charles C.P. Moody, 1857).
185. Mildred F. Hall, "Salem Street Cemetery," *Register of the Malden Historical Society*, vol. 7, 47.
186. Henry Weld Fuller, *The Woodlawn Cemetery in North Chelsea and Malden* (Boston: Higgins and Bradley, 1856); Elizabeth Durfee Hengen, *Life Everlasting: The History, Art, and People of Woodlawn Cemetery, 1850–2000* (Everett, MA: Woodlawn Cemetery, 2001). See also George E. Ellis, *Address Given at the Consecration of Woodlawn Cemetery in Chelsea and Malden* (Boston: John Wilson & Son, 1851).
187. Commager and Cantor, *Documents of American History*, vol. 1, 247.
188. Julia E. Chadwick, "History of the Malden High School," *Catalogue of the Public High School and Alumni Register* (Malden, MA: Geo. E. Dunbar, 1896), 3.
189. Bishop, *Brief Historical Account*, 12. Bishop's history of Lit is also a splendid overview of the history of the high school throughout the 1940s.
190. Ibid., 7.
191. Ibid., 6.

Chapter 6

192. Manisha Sinha, *The Slave's Cause: A History of Abolition* (New Haven: Yale University Press, 2016), 501.
193. Ibid., 527–42.
194. George Prentice, *The Life of Gilbert Haven* (New York: Phillips & Hunt, 1883), 69.
195. Julia Ward Howe, ed., *Representative Women of New England* (Boston: New England Historical Publishing Company, 1904), 283.

196. Charles F. Horner, *The Life of James Redpath* (New York: Barse & Hopkins, 1926), 67; John R. McKivigan, *Forgotten Firebrand: James Redpath and the Making of Nineteenth-Century America* (Ithaca, NY: Cornell University Press, 2008), 43.
197. Mary Lawrence Mann, "Some Notable Women in the Annals of Malden," *Register of the Malden Historical Society*, vol. 2 (Lynn, MA: Frank S. Whitten, 1912), 54, 61; Walter Kendall Watkins, "The Old Morey House," *Register of the Malden Historical Society*, vol. 7 (1967), 64.
198. Loring was a judge of the Suffolk Probate Court and a United States commissioner in the Circuit Court of Massachusetts. As a commissioner, Loring was much reviled for issuing warrants under the Fugitive Slave Act for rendition of fugitive slave Anthony Burns. He was ultimately removed as a probate judge. See Albert J. Von Frank, *The Trials of Anthony Burns: Freedom and Slavery in Emerson's Boston* (Cambridge, MA: Harvard University Press, 1999). There also exists an 1855 petition of Malden residents organized by Herbert Gleason of Oak Grove and signed by the Moreys, seeking the removal of officials who enforce the Fugitive Slave Law.
199. Petition of David B. Morey and 141 other residents of Malden, Massachusetts Anti-Slavery and Anti-Segregation Petitions; House unpassed legislation 1859, rejected SC1/series 230, pages 286–88, Massachusetts Archives. The petition can be viewed at www.http:/nrs.harvard.edu/urn-3:FHCL:11029933.
200. Morey manufactured pewter in partnership with R.H. Ober under the name Morey & Ober and later Morey & Smith. See Kerfoot, *American Pewter*, 169.
201. Mann, "Some Notable Women," 54, 61
202. Watkins, "Old Morey House," 64–65.
203. Howe, *Representative Women of New England*, 283.
204. Ellen Beale Morey quoted in Watkins, "Old Morey House," 66.
205. *Malden City Press*, April 11, 1885.
206. McKivigan, *Forgotten Firebrand*, 43; less satisfactory is Horner, *Life of James Redpath*, as it is more concerned with the lyceum movement and lacks an index.
207. James Redpath, *The Roving Editor, or Talks with Slaves in Southern States* (New York: A.B. Burdick, 1859).
208. The Kansas-Nebraska Act of 1850 nullified the Missouri Compromise of 1820 and mandated that popular sovereignty would determine whether Kansas was free or slave. The state turned into a bloodbath. See Morison and Commager, *Growth of the American Republic*, vol. 1, 622–25.

209. McKivigan, *Forgotten Firebrand*, 37.
210. Ibid., 28–29.
211. Ibid., 29.
212. Ibid., 41, 47.
213. Ibid., 43.
214. Redpath, *Roving Editor*, 86, quoted in McKivigan, *Forgotten Firebrand*, 45.
215. James Redpath, *The Public Life of Capt. John Brown* (Boston: Thayer & Eldridge, 1860).
216. James Redpath, *Echoes of Harper's Ferry* (Boston: Thayer & Eldridge, 1860).
217. McKivigan, *Forgotten Firebrand*, 54.
218. Ibid., 55.
219. Sinha, *Slave's Cause*, 554.
220. Redpath to Thomas Wentworth Higginson, April 20, 1860, quoted in McKivigan, *Forgotten Firebrand*, 56.
221. Horner, *Life of James Redpath*, 71.
222. The Haitian Revolution of 1789, where slaves overthrew the French and established a republic, inspired blacks and abolitionists. See Sinha, *Slave's Cause*, 53–64.
223. Sinha, *Slave's Cause*, 563.
224. Ibid. Quotations in original.
225. Horner, *Life of James Redpath*, 114–15.
226. Ibid., 140–55; McKivigan, *Forgotten Firebrand*, xi and 124.
227. Louisa May Alcott, *Hospital Sketches* (Boston: James Redpath, 1863).
228. McKivigan, *Forgotten Firebrand*, 127.
229. Ibid., 44.
230. Ibid., 128. It is unclear today where "Sunset Rock" was. There are several outcroppings in the area of Redpath's home on Maple Street. It could have been LasCasas's Hill near present-day Francis and Greenleaf Streets (the hill has long been removed), the outcropping on Alpine Street, the rocks behind the old Glenwood School or perhaps even Tea Rock at the Dutton estate.
231. McKivigan, *Forgotten Firebrand*, 128.
232. Ibid., 129.
233. James Redpath, *Talks About Ireland* (New York: P.J. Kenedy, 1881).
234. McKivigan, *Forgotten Firebrand*, xi.
235. The ghostwritten biography was ultimately published by Davis's wife. Varina Davis, *Jefferson Davis, Ex-President of the Confederate States of America: A Memoir by His Wife* (New York: Belford Company, 1890).
236. Quoted in Horner, *Life of James Redpath*, 229.

237. The most recent biography is William B. Gravely, *Gilbert Haven, Methodist Abolitionist: A Study in Race, Religion, and Reform, 1850–1880* (Nashville, TN: Abingdon Press, 1973). See also Prentice, *Life of Gilbert Haven*, and W.H. Daniels, ed., *Memorials of Bishop Gilbert Haven* (Boston: B.B. Russell & Company, 1880).
238. Prentice, *Life of Gilbert Haven*, 22. The account is also reported in Daniels, *Memorials of Bishop Gilbert Haven*, 27.
239. Prentice, *Life of Gilbert Haven*, 22.
240. Ibid., 299.
241. Gravely, *Gilbert Haven, Methodist Abolitionist*, 120.
242. Ibid., 107.
243. Daniels, *Memorials of Bishop Gilbert Haven*, 259.
244. Ibid., 61.
245. Ibid., 41.
246. Gilbert Haven, "The Higher Law," extract from the sermon in Daniels, *Memorials of Bishop Gilbert Haven*, 322. The entire sermon is reproduced in Gilbert Haven, *National Sermons: Sermons, Speeches, and Letters on Slavery and Its War* (Boston: Lee & Shepard, 1869).
247. Daniels, *Memorials of Bishop Gilbert Haven*, 59.
248. Gravely, *Gilbert Haven, Methodist Abolitionist*, 49.
249. Ibid., 119.
250. Ibid., 110.
251. Ibid.
252. Prentice, *Life of Gilbert Haven*, 336.
253. Ibid., 468.
254. Ibid.
255. Haven, *National Sermons*. Haven also authored two travelogues: *The Pilgrim's Wallet* (New York: Hurd and Houghton, 1866), a record of his 1862 European tour, and *Our Next-Door Neighbor: A Winter in Mexico* (New York: Harper & Bros., 1875), an account of his travels in Mexico.
256. Daniels, *Memorials of Bishop Gilbert Haven*, 183; Gravely, *Gilbert Haven, Methodist Abolitionist*, 250.
257. Prentice, *Life of Gilbert Haven*, 511.

Chapter 7

258. Thomas Kirwan and Henry Splaine, *Memorial History of the Seventeenth Regiment Massachusetts Volunteer Infantry (Old and New Organizations) in the Civil*

War from 1861–1865 (Salem, MA: Salem Press Company, 1911), 61–62. Malden men also served in other companies of the 17th Regiment. Mary Waterman Perry, *Malden, Massachusetts in the Civil War* 10 (1935), mss. in possession of Malden Historical Society. Additionally, after a call for volunteers in 1862, forty-three Malden men were enlisted in the 43rd and 44th Regiments. Perry, *Malden, Massachusetts in the Civil War*, 3, 11–12.

259. Walton S. Hall, "First Civil War Casualty," *Register of the Malden Historical Society*, vol. 7 (1967), 86.

260. Perry, *Malden, Massachusetts in the Civil War*, 2.

261. Ibid., 3.

262. Sergeant Henry Foskett, Corporal James R. Gilchrist and Privates Charles M. Eagan, Oscar Biebier, Thomas H. Speed, Albert W. Crockett and James M. Powers. See Perry, *Malden, Massachusetts in the Civil War*, 5.

263. Leverett D. Holden, *My First and Last Fights* (Malden, MA: Samuel Tilden, 1914), 9.

264. *Memorial RGS* (Cambridge, MA: University Press, 1864), 29; Sarah Greenough and Nancy K. Anderson, *Tell It with Pride: The 54th Massachusetts Regiment and Augustus Saint-Gaudens' Shaw Memorial* (New Haven, CT: Yale University Press, 2013), 166.

265. Luis F. Emilio, *History of the Fifty-Fourth Regiment of Massachusetts Volunteer Infantry, 1863–1865* (Boston: Boston Book Company, 1891), 81, 92.

266. Ibid., 165.

267. Ibid., 183.

268. Ibid., 288.

269. A second Medal of Honor recipient is also buried in Malden at the Holy Cross Cemetery. Sergeant Richard P. Hanley received the Medal of Honor for service in the Battle of Little Bighorn in 1876. See *Boston Globe*, "After 140 Years, Malden Grave of Little-Known Soldier Gets a Tribute," June 14, 2016.

270. See Perry, *Malden, Massachusetts in the Civil War*, 6, which states that 832 served.

271. Records of the Ladies' Soldiers Aid Society, October 15, 1862, in possession of the Malden Historical Society. See also Walton S. Hall, "Soldiers' Aid Society," *Register of the Malden Historical Society*, vol. 7 (1967), 83.

272. Georgianna Brown Mirick (class of 1865). See *Catalogue of the Public High School and Alumni Register* (Malden, MA: Geo. E. Dunbar, 1896), 20.

273. Journal of the Malden High School, commencing April 13, 1864, entry for April 17, 1865. The journals are in the possession of the Malden

Historical Society. The high school journals are a remarkable, untapped resource. From September 1, 1862, to July 3, 1881, they give a daily chronicle of high school life in the mid-nineteenth century. Entries were written daily by students.

274. Ibid., entry for April 11, 1865.
275. Lizzie L. Collins (class of 1866). See *Catalogue of the Public High School and Alumni Register*, 20.
276. Journal of the Malden High School, entry for April 17, 1865.
277. Ibid., entry for April 18, 1865.

Chapter 8

278. Many of the contemporary press reports, the Redpath book, Governor Andrew's opinion to the council and some court records are collected in Steven Capfield, ed., *It Took a Village: The Lynching of Edward Green for the Death of Frank Converse* (Boston: Steven Capfield d/b/a Capfield's Press, 2007).
279. Hearing before Charlestown Police Court, testimony of Henry Stone, reported in *Boston Journal*, January 7, 1864.
280. Diary of Fred Hadley, mss in possession of Malden Historical Society.
281. *Boston Journal*, December 16, 1863.
282. Journal of the Malden High School, entry for December 15, 1863.
283. The award was ultimately shared by A.D. Lamson ($125), M.S. Shedd ($100), Caleb Waite ($100), George D.B. Blanchard ($50), J.H. Abbott ($50), Charles H. Sprague ($50) and Hubbard Russell ($25). Malden Town Report, 1864.
284. *Boston Journal*, January 8, 1864.
285. Ibid., February 8, 1864; *New York Times*, February 9, 1864.
286. Personal conversation with the late Miss Dorathy Rothe.
287. *The Life, Character, and Career of Edward W. Green: Postmaster of Malden, the Murderer of Frank E. Converse* (Boston: Benjamin B. Russell, 1864).
288. John Davidson, *A Tribute to the Memory of Frank Eugene Converse, Aged 17 Years, Who Was Assassinated in the Bank of Malden, December 15, 1863* ([Malden?], n.d.), n.p.
289. McKivigan, *Forgotten Firebrand*, 94.
290. Henry Greenleaf Pearson, *The Life of John A. Andrew, Governor of Massachusetts, 1861–1865*, vol. 2 (Boston: Houghton, Mifflin & Company, 1904) 219.
291. *Boston Journal*, April 26, 1864.

292. A Citizen of Malden [James Redpath], *Shall We Suffocate Ed. Green?* (Boston: James Redpath, 1864).
293. Prentice, *Life of Gilbert Haven*, 306–8.
294. McKivigan, *Forgotten Firebrand*, 95.
295. Pearson, *Life of John A. Andrew*, vol. 2, 219.
296. *Boston Journal*, June 2, 1864.
297. Ibid., May 16, 1864. At least that was the "understanding" of the person offering the testimony.
298. Ibid., November 3, 1864.
299. *Opinion of the Justices*, 91 Mass. (9 Allen) 585 (1864).
300. Pearson, *Life of John A. Andrew*, vol. 2, 220.
301. Ibid.
302. *Boston Journal*, February 11, 1865.
303. Pearson, *Life of John A. Andrew*, vol. 2, 221.
304. Ibid., 225.
305. John A. Andrew, *Governor Andrew's Opinion in the Case of Edward W. Green* (Boston, 1866).
306. Pearson, *Life of John A. Andrew*, vol. 2, 224.
307. Message of Governor Alexander Bullock, February 27, 1866, in Capfield, *It Took a Village*, 223–32.
308. Pearson, *Life of John A. Andrew*, vol. 2, 225.
309. *Green v. Commonwealth*, 94 Mass. (12 Allen) 155 (1866); Pearson, *Life of John A. Andrew*, vol. 2, 226.
310. *Boston Journal*, April 11, 1866.
311. Ibid., April 14, 1866. In 1867, Green's widow, Clara Green, was engaged to be remarried to John William Chapman, a well-regarded Boston attorney. Tragedy befell Clara again, as her husband-to-be was killed in a train wreck. Charity Ann Vogel, *The Angola Horror: The 1867 Train Wreck that Shocked the Nation and Transformed American Railroads* (Ithaca, NY: Cornell University Press, 2013), 45, 106.

Chapter 9

312. Bailey, "Everett: A Historical Sketch," 22.
313. Ibid., 22–23.
314. Ibid., 37; Elizabeth Durfee Hengen, *Building the City of Homes and Industry: The Architectural and Historical Development of Everett, Massachusetts* (Everett, MA: Daniels Printing Company, 1994), 9.

315. William Pellisier, "Old Malden," *Register of the Malden Historical Society*, vol. 7 (1967), 28.
316. Malden Town Report, 1872.
317. *Annual Report of the Town of Malden, March 1, 1858—March 1, 1859* (Boston: C.C.P. Moody, 1859), 10–11.
318. See *Annual Report of the Town of Malden for the Year Ending March 1, 1863* (five watchmen); *Annual Report of the Town of Malden for the Year Ending February 28, 1870* (four night police).
319. *Malden Mirror*, March 28, 1874.
320. *Reports of the Town Officers of Malden for the Year Ending December 31, 1875* (Boston: Rand, Avery & Company, 1876), 7.
321. *Malden Mirror*, March 6, 1876.
322. Frank F. Russell, "The Forgotten Sacrifice of David S. Faulkner," *Sandy Bank Sentinel: The Journal of the Malden Historical Society* 6, no. 4 (Autumn 2001): 5.
323. Malden Town Report, 1872.
324. Ruth L.S. Child, *Chronicle of the Malden High School Library* (n.p., 1915), 11–12.
325. Irving S. Cole, "Historical Sketch of the Malden Public Library," *Register of the Malden Historical Society*, vol. 7 (1967), 15.
326. Appreciation, interpretation and criticism of the library's architecture may be found most recently in Kenneth A. Breisch, *Henry Hobson Richardson and the Small Public Library in America* (Cambridge, MA: MIT Press, 1997), 190–217. The classic work on Richardson's architecture remains Mariana Griswold Van Rensselaer, *Henry Hobson Richardson and His Works* (Boston: Houghton, Mifflin & Company, 1888).
327. Breisch, *Henry Hobson Richardson*, 39.
328. Ibid.
329. Ibid., 198.
330. Personal communication with library trustee, Dr. John Tramondozzi.
331. Breisch, *Henry Hobson Richardson*, 204. The intended transformational experience is now lost, however, as the library trustees have closed the original entrance with the opening of the 1996 library addition.
332. *Dedication of the Converse Memorial Building* (Boston: Alfred Mudge & Son, 1886), 9.
333. *In Memory of Elisha Slade Converse*, 5–6.
334. Medford was later removed from the jurisdiction of the Malden District Court.
335. Cummings, "Horse Car Days," 21.

336. Paul, *Linden on the Saugus Branch*, 5–6.
337. Cummings, "Horse Car Days," 21, but see also Pellisier, "Old Malden," 28.

Chapter 10

338. *Malden Mirror*, June 4, 1881, 1.
339. Ibid.
340. *Malden Press*, June 4, 1881, 4.
341. Ibid.
342. Ibid.
343. *Malden Mirror*, June 11, 1881, 1.
344. *Malden City Press*, June 11, 1881, 4.
345. Ibid.
346. Converse received 1,521 of the 1,550 votes cast for mayor. *Malden Mirror*, December 3, 1881. For a discussion of Malden politics at the time, see Walton S. Hall, "Political Intelligence Then and Now," MA thesis, Boston University, 1931, available at www.archive.org/details/politicalintelli00hall.
347. In 1908, a special act of the legislature reduced the school committee to five members and divested the mayor of his involvement.
348. *Views of Malden, Mass.* (Portland, ME: L.H. Nelson, 1902).
349. Ibid.
350. Claire Dutton McGregor Matz, *Glen Rock and the Dutton Girls* (n.p.: privately printed, 1976). See also Joseph Crook Anderson II, *The Duttons of Glen Rock, Malden, Massachusetts* (Baltimore, MD: Otter Bay Books, 2013), 7–27.
351. *Souvenir Views of Malden, Mass.* (Malden, MA: Eugene A. Perry, 1896).
352. John P. Merrill and Suzanne Merrill, eds., *Squirrel Island, Maine: The First Hundred Years* (Freeport, ME: Bond Wheelwright Company, 1971), 9–11.
353. Ezra G. Perry, *A Trip Around Buzzards Bay Shores* (reprint, Taunton, MA: Bourne Historical Commission/William S. Sullwood, 1976), 65, photographs 68, 70.
354. Ibid., 255, photograph 260.
355. *Souvenir History of Malden, Mass.* (Everett, MA: Frank D. Woodbury, 1899), 11.
356. Ibid., 12.

357. Anna Christy Fall, "Views of Malden Not Often Seen," *Carnival of Nations in Aid of the Malden Hospital Souvenir* (Boston: C.B. Webster, 1894), 101. Her daughter, Emma Fall Schofield, went on to become the first female judge in Massachusetts.

Chapter 11

358. *Malden Past and Present* (Malden, MA: Malden Mirror, 1899), 17–19.
359. Horace Robbins Burdick, "My Book," *Register of the Malden Historical Society*, vol. 9 (1984), 9, 63.
360. Ibid.
361. Ibid., 64.
362. *Register of the Malden Historical Society*, vol. 9, 92.
363. Nancy Allyn Jarzombek, *The Glow of Sunlight: Paintings by George L. Noyes*, catalogue for exhibition at Vose Galleries, Boston, October 13–November 28, 1998.
364. *Artist's Exhibition and Sale in the Gallery of C.O. Elliett* (1897). A copy can be seen at www.archive.org/details/COElliettArtistsExhibitionandSale1897.
365. See entry "A.H. Davenport Co." in Doreen Bolger Burke, et al., *In Pursuit of Beauty: Americans and the Aesthetic Movement* (New York: Rizzoli, 1986), 418.
366. See Anne Farnum, "A.H. Davenport and Company Boston Furniture Makers," *Magazine Antiques* 109 (May 1976): 1,048–55.

Chapter 12

367. Sylvester Baxter, "The Parks of Malden," *Carnival of Nations in Aid of the Malden Hospital Souvenir*, 33.
368. Ibid.
369. Ibid.
370. [Sylvester Baxter], "Sylvester Baxter," in James Phinney Baxter, *The Baxter Family: A Collection of Genealogies* (N.p., 1921), 94–102. See also Cynthia Zaitzevsky, "Sylvester Baxter," in Charles A. Birnbaum and Robin S. Karson, eds., *Pioneers of American Landscape Design* (New York: McGraw Hill, 2000), 19–21.
371. Sylvester Baxter, *Plastic Sketches of J.G. and J.F. Low* (Boston: Lee and Shephard, 1887).

372. Sylvester Baxter, *The Morse Collection of Japanese Pottery* (Salem, MA: Essex Institute, 1887).
373. Sylvester Baxter, "An American Palace of Art," *Century Magazine* 67, no. 3 (January 1904): 362–82.
374. Sylvester Baxter, "The German Way of Making Better Cities," *Atlantic Monthly* (July 1909): 72–95.
375. Sylvester Baxter, *Greater Boston: A Study for a Federalized Metropolis Comprising the City of Boston and Surrounding Cities and Towns* (Boston: A.J. Philpott & Company, 1891). Baxter pioneered use of the term "Greater Boston."
376. Sylvester Baxter, "Walt Whitman in Boston," *New England Magazine* 6 (August 1892): 714–21.
377. Sylvester Baxter, *Spanish Colonial Architecture in Mexico*, with photographic plates by Henry Greenwood Peabody and plans by Bertram Grosvenor Goodhue (Boston: J.B. Millett, 1901).
378. Curtis M. Hinsley, ed., *The Southwest in the American Imagination: The Writings of Sylvester Baxter, 1881–1889* (Tucson: University of Arizona Press, 1996).
379. William B. deLasCasas, "The Metropolitan Parks," *Carnival of Nations in Aid of the Malden Hospital Souvenir*, 43.
380. *Appalachia* 2 no. 2 (July 1880): 198–99; William B. deLasCasas, "The Middlesex Fells," *New England Magazine* 18, no. 6 (August 1898): 702–3.
381. *Report of the Board of Metropolitan Park Commissioners: Boston Metropolitan Park Report* (Boston, 1893).
382. Sylvester Baxter, *Boston Park Guide, Including the Municipal and Metropolitan Systems of Greater Boston* (Boston: Small Maynard & Company, 1898).
383. Baxter, "Parks of Malden," 33.
384. Ibid.
385. Ibid., 33–35.
386. Search of Olmsted Associates records, 1863–1971, online at loc.gov. For some information on some of the parks, see *Register of the Malden Historical Society*, vol. 1 (Lynn, MA: Frank S. Whitten, 1910), 5–21; Malden Historical Society, *Bell Rock Memorial Park* (Malden, MA: Kernwood/Forbes Press, 2000); Inna Babitskaya, *Fellsmere Park—Emerald of Malden* (Malden, MA: privately published, 2012).
387. Breisch, *Henry Hobson Richardson*, 198.
388. Claudia L. Bushman, *A Good Poor Man's Wife: Being a Chronicle of Harriet Hanson Robinson and Her Family in Nineteenth Century New England* (Hanover, NH: University Press of New England, 1981), 93. Both Harriet Hanson Robinson and her daughter, Harriette Lucy Robinson

Shattuck, are fascinating examples of the changing role of women in the nineteenth century. Their prolific diaries and scrapbooks are collected in the Schlesinger Library on the History of Women at Radcliffe Institute, Harvard University, Cambridge. For an account of Harriet's transformative year of 1870, see Claudia L. Bushman, *Going to Boston: Harriet Robinson's Journey to New Womanhood* (Hanover, NH: University Press of New England, 2017). See also Bernice Selden, *The Mills Girls: Lucy Larcom, Harriet Hanson Robinson, Sarah G. Bagley* (New York: Atheneum, 1983).

389. Bushman, *Good Poor Man's Wife*, 88.

390. For William Robinson's writings, see Harriet Hanson Robinson, ed., *"Warrington" Pen-Portraits: A Collection of Personal and Political Reminiscences from 1848 to 1876* (Boston: Lee and Shepard, 1877).

391. Ibid., 157.

392. Ibid., 52, 158.

393. Ibid., 25.

394. Harriet Hanson Robinson, *Massachusetts in the Woman Suffrage Movement* (Boston: Roberts Brothers, 1881), 219–20. The year of the convention is given as 1876 on page 59 of Robinson's history.

395. Ibid., 220–21.

396. Ruth Kimball Randall, *Old and New: Recollections of Ninety-Five Years, 1878–1973* (Malden, MA), 1–3.

397. Ibid., 4–5; Adeline A. Nichols, "The Old and New," *Carnival of Nations in Aid of the Malden Hospital Souvenir*, 91.

398. Randall, *Old and New*, 11.

399. Women were allowed to serve on school committees in Massachusetts beginning in 1874.

400. E. Gertrude Copeland, "The Enterprise Club," *Carnival of Nations in Aid of the Malden Hospital Souvenir*, 93.

401. Randall, *Old and New*, 13; Anna Christy Fall, *The Tragedy of a Widow's Third* (Boston: I.P. Fox, 1898).

402. Readers interested in these movements should consult the classic work Richard Hofstadter, *The Age of Reform* (New York: Alfred A. Knopf, 1955), especially chapters 2 and 5. There were many subtle distinctions between populism, socialism, nationalism and progressivism.

403. For a brief biography of Winn, see "Henry Winn," *Massachusetts of To-Day* (Boston: Columbia Publishing Company, 1892), 418. The volume also contains a biography of Pierce.

404. *Malden Mirror*, December 3, 1892.

405. *New Nation*, November 26, 1892, 699.
406. *Boston Daily Index*, quoted in "The Malden Election," *New Nation*, December 24, 1892, 758.
407. Sylvester Baxter, "The Author of Looking Backward," in Edward Bellamy, *Looking Backward, 2000–1887* (New York: Grosset & Dunlap, 1898).
408. Sylvester Baxter, "Why the Name, Nationalism?," *The Nationalist* 1, no. 3 (July 1889): 82–83. See also Sylvester Baxter, "What Is Nationalism," *The Nationalist* 1, no. 1 (May 1889): 8–12.
409. Cyrus Field Willard, "The Nationalist Club of Boston," *The Nationalist* 1, no. 1 (May 1899): 16–20; Arthur Lipow, *Authoritarian Socialism in America: Edward Bellamy and the Nationalist Movement* (Berkeley: University of California Press, 1982), 123–24.
410. *General Report of the Thirteenth Convention and Anniversary of the Theosophical Society* (1888), 80. Also see entry for George David Ayers in *Harvard College Class of 1879 Secretary's Report* (1895), 23–24.
411. J. Gordon Melton, "Theosophical Communities and Their Ideal of Universal Brotherhood," in Donald E. Pitzer, ed., *America's Communal Utopias* (Chapel Hill: University of North Carolina Press, 1997), 396–99.

Chapter 13

412. Dana J. Flanders, "The Kernwood Club," *Carnival of Nations in Aid of the Malden Hospital Souvenir*, 23.
413. William H. Winship, "A History of the Kernwood Club," *Kernwood Club Golden Anniversary, 1889–1939* (Malden, MA: Kernwood Club, 1939), 7–11.
414. Ibid., 14–15.
415. Ibid., 15, 46.
416. Ibid., 15–19.
417. Bishop, *Brief Historical Account*, 12.
418. Frank F. Russell, "Some Notes on the Pine Banks Golf Club," *Sandy Bank Sentinel: The Journal of the Malden Historical Society* (Winter 2017): 3.
419. *W.A. Greenough's Directory of the City of Malden* (Boston: W.A. Greenough, 1882), 203.
420. Dexter Allis, "The Belmont Bikers, 1896–1899," *Register of the Malden Historical Society*, vol. 7 (1967), 33–40; Lorenz J. Finison, *Boston's Cycling Craze, 1880–1900* (Amherst: University of Massachusetts Press, 2014), 187–91.

421. Finison, *Boston's Cycling Craze*, 114–15.
422. *Sandy Bank Sentinel: The Journal of the Malden Historical Society* (Fall 1998).
423. F.S.A., "A Football Prospectus," *The Oracle* 7, no. 1 (September 20, 1894): 2.
424. The first four are, in order, 1875—Norwich Free Academy (Norwich, CT) versus New London High School (New London, CT); 1882—Wellesley High School (Wellesley, MA) versus Needham High School (Needham, MA); 1883—Fordham Preparatory School (Bronx, NY) versus Xavier High School (New York, NY); and 1887—Boston Latin School (Boston, MA) versus English High School (Boston, MA). Retrieved from www.mitchellandness.com.
425. MHS had an ice polo team when the sport was ascendant in the mid-1890s. See *The Oracle*, February 7, 1895, 5.
426. David Hackett Fischer, *Liberty and Freedom: A Visual History of America's Founding Ideas* (Oxford, UK: Oxford University Press, 2005), 406.
427. Jeffrey Owen Jones and Peter Meyer, *The Pledge: A History of the Pledge of Allegiance* (New York: Macmillan, 2010), 100.
428. *The Youth's Companion*, September 8, 1892, 446.
429. Francis Bellamy, "The Story of the Pledge of Allegiance to the Flag," *University of Rochester Library Bulletin* 8, no. 2 (Winter 1953).
430. Margarette S. Miller, *Twenty-Three Words* (reprint, n.p.: Printcraft Press, 1976).
431. Jones and Meyer, *The Pledge*, 101–5.
432. Massachusetts House of Representatives, House Resolution no. 2644 (1956).
433. Jones and Meyer, *The Pledge*, 107.
434. *Time and the Hour* 9, no. 25, "Some Old Towns, II: Malden" (May 27, 1899).
435. *Memorial of the Celebration of the Two Hundred and Fiftieth Anniversary*, 178.
436. Ibid., 186, 253.
437. Ibid., 179–85.

INDEX

J

K

L

M

N

O

P

ABOUT THE AUTHOR

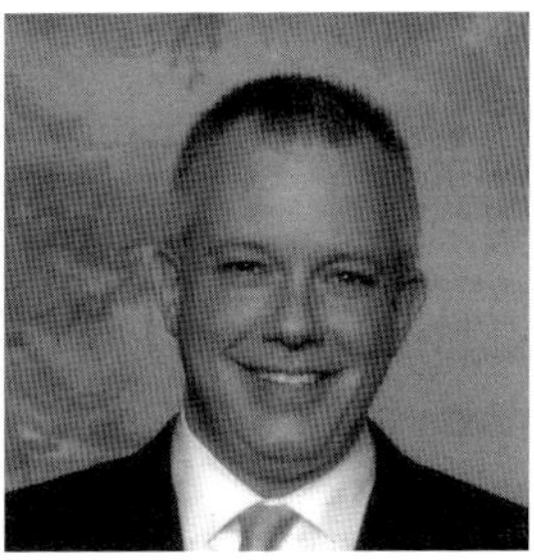

Frank F. Russell is a lifelong Malden resident. He graduated from Malden High School and earned a BA in history from the University of Massachusetts–Amherst and a JD from Suffolk University Law School. He is a former member of the Malden School Committee. He has served on several boards of community organizations. He is a past president of the Malden Historical Society, for which he continues to edit its newsletter. He is the father of two children, Madison and Edwin.

Visit us at
www.historypress.com